I0108115

THE NO
FLUFF
ZONE

The Trailer into Success

JAYLA EMBABY

The No Fluff Zone

Copyright © 2024 by Jayla Embaby.

All rights reserved. No part of this publication may be reproduced, distributed, or transmitted in any form or by any means, including photocopying, recording, or other electronic or mechanical methods, without the written consent of the publisher. The only exceptions are for brief quotations included in critical reviews and other noncommercial uses permitted by copyright law.

MILTON & HUGO L.L.C.
4407 Park Ave., Suite 5
Union City, NJ 07087, USA

Website: *www. miltonandhugo.com*
Hotline: *1- 888-778-0033*
Email: *info@miltonandhugo.com*

Ordering Information:
Quantity sales. Special discounts are granted to corporations, associations, and other organizations. For more information on these discounts, please reach out to the publisher using the contact information provided above.

Library of Congress Control Number:		2024917134
ISBN-13:	979-8-89285-252-4	[Paperback Edition]
	979-8-89285-254-8	[Hardback Edition]
	979-8-89285-251-7	[Digital Edition]

Rev. date: 09/13/2024

CONTENTS

INTRODUCTION

Before I begin, take out a pen or highlighter. I want you to underline, circle, note, or jot down anything that stands out to you while reading.

We learn most when we emphasize, re-read, or re-think about things that stand out to us, so please do so. I want this book to bring the most value to you, and it will.

I'm about to spill some serious tea in this book! If you don't know what that means, it basically just means "sharing a secret or some really interesting information", which again, I will be. I'm going to share my personal experiences of what I have gone through and use it to highlight the highs and the lows of what happened and how I got out of these situations as well. I will be doing this by sharing my experiences, stories, as well as those of others who taught me an abundance and made my perspective shift.

In this book I will help you see life from another perspective, to change your mindset to a growth mindset rather than a fixed mindset.

I personally believe we learn the most from our worst experiences as well as our deep conversations with others. When we are under the most stress that's how we truly know who we are, and we can be aware and build from there.

When we talk to others, we get more insight from experiences they have been through that we have not as well as learn from their shared experiences. That's what all knowledge collected in the past billions of trillions of years is right? People's past experiences and stories, that's what we are taught in school, and we learn from it. We see what people in the past have done and where they went wrong and do our best not to repeat it.

For those of you who don't know what those mindsets are, a growth mindset is ideally a mindset that you are always wanting to be better and grow, whereas in a fixed mindset you are just staying where you are without the need, want, reason, or motivation to grow.

Well, you probably want to know who I am. My name is Jayla Embaby and I'm 21 years old – well 21 when I started writing this book on September 4th, 2022! Who knows how old I will be when it's finished?! In my conclusion, I will put the finished date. Life is really hectic and I'm excessively busy, but time is created, not found. I was born December 27, 2001 in Minnesota. My whole family originated from Cairo, Egypt. When I was eight years old, I moved to Arizona and have been living here ever since. My life has been pretty smooth sailing for the most part, with a lot of large hurdles along the way. As I begin writing this book, I have decided that I am going to start journaling, meditating, and jotting down notes as I continue to improve myself, my wellbeing as well as all the hectic events life throws my way. I want to help you, and I can't help others without helping myself first.

My hope is that I can help show how I get through my days with the mindset I have. Hopefully as I use these self-growth tools, I can experiment with what has worked best, what has not, and what I've learned in the process of writing this for all of you. You will gain great perspective, tips, and motivation from reading this book and it will encourage you to attribute these tactics into your everyday life as well.

THE START OF SUCCESS

This is going to sound very cliché but a lot of the motivation I have is driven from my mom. You see, my dad passed when I was 4 years old, so my mom and I moved to Arizona when I was 8. It wasn't just for a better life and schooling, but to be with my Aunt Dina (My mom's sister- I call her Didi) and her two kids Layla and Zane. When my Uncle Sam and my Didi divorced, my mom and aunt got a house together to raise their kids together, leading us to then having our own extended, blended, and nontraditional family that I value so much. Growing up every year on Father's Day I would get so upset and down. Year after year, seeing all the advertisements for Father's Day gifts was difficult in addition to school events such as Daddy Daughter dances or Donuts for Dads. It made me sad and wonder why this happened to me.

As I grew up it became more bearable, and I've become more accepting of the fact my Dad is gone – and that's okay. The closest person I would say to a Dad, is my Uncle Sam, the father of Layla and Zane. He has always opened his home to me growing up, is always there for the big life transitioning events, as well as been there when I needed help or advice. Knowing that, I have also had Didi, my aunt. Although, Didi is something different. Not only is she one of smartest women I know, she is also the most efficient and quick woman when it comes to shopping for weekly groceries and cooking our nightly family dinners, the most productive woman when it comes to planning the weekdays for what needs to get done, and the toughest woman I know, voicing her opinion and not letting anyone walk over hers. She's very loyal so if you wrong her, it will take ALOT to get her trust back.

I believe that watching her while growing up, I developed a need for always wanting to get things done. I would like to say I'm highly productive and that came from her. She uses her time wisely, she writes down what she needs to do in a day on the notes app on her phone, not a calendar, and erases it off the list when she completes it. I took that from her, and I have gotten so much stuff done that I had not gotten done vs just referring back to my planner.

Now my mom is pretty opposite. She is smart, just like Didi, and she gets things done but on her own time. She has a schedule, but she isn't in a rush, she makes the time. My mom is very social and extroverted, she is unbiased when it comes to rising problems, and really good at seeing others perspectives on situations.

The one thing that both my Mom and Didi have in common is they are funny and know how to make fun of any situation life throws their way. I have watched them go from nothing to everything, with the mindset that it would get better. Of course, they had their moments of weakness where they would break down, but everyone does and it's human. They were each other's support system, when one was down the other was there to help and likewise.

Watching them going from nothing to everything really made me realize that no matter the struggle in life, it's doable. Whatever I'm going through, it will pass. I just need to walk right through it, learn from it, and come out stronger and more knowledgeable than before. Whatever it is I ended up going through, I can learn information from the situation to prevent it from happening again, and if it happens again, I will know how to get out of it because I already went through it.

Mom and Aunt Didi can take any stressful situation and make it more lighthearted and just laugh. One of the most amazing things about growing up with my mom and Didi as my primary caregivers, was watching them overcome hurdles with communication. I watched how they raised a family together and not let it strain the relationship between each other as sisters, and that is beautiful.

That being said, Didi is not just my aunt, but she is my Mom. She's been there for me, mentored me, guided, encouraged, and motivated me, just like a mom. Overtime I have realized that I'm so blessed to have grown up with two of the strongest women in my life as my mentors and caregivers. They went against the social norms of men and women. They showed me that you do not need a man to be successful and have nice cars, a big house, a family, a dog, a pool, a nice living room and kitchen and the list goes on. They challenged this social norm and proved that it was possible, and you can accomplish anything with commitment, hard work, and consistency. And that's exactly what I'm going to do!

CHAPTER

1

MOTIVATION

Some days are harder than others. But I have grown up to realize that you must have the bad days in order to appreciate the good ones.

It wasn't until I traveled back to Egypt for the first time in 13 years that I felt so grateful for the life my mom has provided for me here in the U.S. I had just turned 21 a few months before and I still lived with my mom while I attended school full time at Arizona State University as well as worked part-time as a server at IHOP.

I have been a server at IHOP for 3 years now and absolutely love it. It can be really stressful sometimes but it's manageable. I think some days I want to leave but the one thing keeping me there right now is my family.

You see, my mom got laid off from her job a little bit before my birthday, so I had offered to step up. Instead of putting my tips I make in my savings account, I gave it to my mom to help with expenses. She was very hesitant about it and did not like the idea at all. I didn't understand why because she is my mom, but she had finally come to terms with the fact I was not going to take no for an answer.

It's important to realize that motivation comes from a MOTIVE, a reason, and overall a WHY. WHY are you doing what you're doing? WHY do you want to achieve that goal? If your reason WHY you do something is strong enough, it will push you to show up day in and day out to achieve it. It's something that moves you to want to do it, that's why it's so important to figure out why you want to do or be something.

For example, if you wanted to start going to the gym to gain muscle and look leaner, that is what motivates you to show up to the gym day in and day out and eat better. You have a why, you have a goal in mind, so you are more moved to reach it.

I feel that so many aspects of my life have gotten better or made me stronger because of this. I know how weird it is to say that my mom losing her job has actually helped me. But it's true. For example, I made an exceedingly large amount of tips because of the fact my mindset has changed from "ugh another table" to "Do it for mama".

Just like I stated earlier, this was a hard time for me, but we see who we truly are under stressful situations. My "why" became so big because all I wanted to do was relieve the stress and any negative emotion my mom had in any way I could, and if that required me to push a little harder and be happy around her for her, it's what I was going to do, no questions asked.

On top of it all, it also helped me in my fitness and health journey. I worked even harder in the gym so I could show my younger cousin Layla (who I call my sister because she basically is) that your focus in the gym can show tremendous effects physically and mentally. Plus showing my mom that eating healthy doesn't mean you have to cut down on the foods you love, but just eating smaller portions in moderation and doing something small like taking a 30 minute walk a day changes a lot.

Many people don't realize that the way they look at something is a game changer. If you look at going to the gym as a chore, then you are most likely not going to want to do it. Change your words in everything you do from "I have to do this" to "I get to do this". It's really refreshing sometimes to sit back and realize how blessed you are to have all the things you do in life.

Sometimes your motivation could be to inspire others. Whoever it may be, show them that you truly are capable of anything, and you can achieve and get anything done no matter what. When we see others getting things done regardless of the hardships going on in their life, it has us reflect on our own life and hardships. We then start to question ourselves in ways such as "If this person can do all of that and go through a hard time, I can too". Having someone show you that it is truly possible can be motivating in itself.

That's why it's so important to be aware of what kind of people you are surrounding yourself with in your life as well. Being around hardworking, disciplined, motivated, committed, successful people will push you to have the same outlook and do those same things as well. On the contrary, if you are around people who just play video games all day, are lazy and unmotivated, you will not have a desire to push yourself. You will participate in the same behaviors of those who you surround yourself with.

This situation also sparked some change in me. It motivated me to want to grow, do more, and be better. Not just for myself but the people around me. It made me realize that changing to better yourself will in return help the others around you as well.

THE LITTLE MINDSET CHANGES

If you just take that one little step, just change your perspective, the rest of the steps will soon follow to support your goals. How is that so you may ask? Well let's look at one example I shared earlier: When I wasn't in need of the money as much as I am now, every time I got a new table, I would think to myself "Ugh another table" or "They sat me again?" or even "I just want to go home, does anybody want this table?"

Because I was thinking that way, my mind has then convinced my body that I don't even want to work. So that's then going to make me not only

3

unmotivated to take the tables, but probably lead to me taking a while to get to them, get their drinks, remember condiments they asked for, because I already classified in my head that this table is unimportant to me.

When something is unimportant to you, you're not going to prioritize things in your head you find beneficial to you. When I did shift my perspective because of my situation this is how the voices started to sound in my head:

"Yes I got it!" or "I got sat again? Perfect, I'll be right there!" or even "I can take that table if you don't want it!" I'd like to say I had a "Do it for Mama" mentality every time I got a table. I had a rush of determination, accountability, efficiency, and productivity that stayed consistent with me throughout the shift. Why is that?

Because I had a goal to reach, I had an end game in mind that pushed me to get to a particular outcome. Before I was just saving money meaninglessly without a specific drive. This idea that you need an end goal in mind is key to many factors in life. You have to want to be better, you have to want to succeed, you have to want to finish. If you're just doing something day in and day out or just going with the flow, you will never grow or get better. You need to have goals in life to push you further and further so you can unlock the most unimaginable amazing version of yourself. When you shift your mindset from a negative state of mind to a positive state of mind, whatever goal you set in place that you want to achieve will be achieved. Your mind is the greatest thing that holds you back, so take control of it! Stop overthinking! Either do it or don't do it! Stop wasting time thinking and take action!

MEDITATION

Meditation is one of the strategies that I have found really helps me get through my day. I wake up and meditate for 10 minutes a day. If you are just starting out, 5 minutes a day should do the trick.

Something I did that helped me start meditating is I searched up on Spotify: "5 minute meditation for stress" There would be multiple results that would come up. I would then just press play and listen to the guided meditation in a seated position with my eyes closed. I would just search up a 5-minute meditation for whatever emotion I was feeling that day, stressed, angry, self-doubt, overthinking, anxiety. Any emotion you are feeling search up the 5 minute meditation for it and it helps. Just start now, there is no better time to start anything in life than right now.

I have struggled my whole life with overthinking, having anxiety, and stressing about little things that didn't need to be stressed about. When I started meditating 5 minutes a day I noticed a huge shift in my energy. I noticed that meditation helped me most when I would get into an argument with someone. Oftentimes I used to get upset, not listen, and get all worked up and would just cut people off. Now I am able to just listen. I notice if the person I'm arguing with is getting frustrated or starts raising their voice at me. If they are, I simply tell them that their tone of voice is rude and unnecessary, and they can still get their point across without raising their voice or talking down to me.

Meditation brings a sense of calmness and grounding, it gives your brain a minute to stop thinking of all the stuff you want and still need to do, and to just focus on your breath. When you focus on something such as your breathing, it lets all the thoughts that are there in your mind scrambling around settle and fall back down from the crazy tornado of thoughts in your head.

Let me put it in perspective for you, our minds are like a snow globe. When we are constantly shaking the snow globe, the snow is flying everywhere. Although, the minute we stop shaking it the snow settles all back down to the bottom of the globe and you can see clearly through the globe without all the snowflakes everywhere. Our minds are the same way.

That's why meditating and helping yourself mentally will ideally help others around you too. The minute you shift the greater good, it shifts everyone else around you too. Meditating does nothing but benefit you, so why wouldn't you start doing it and start doing it now? It takes 5 minutes out of your day. 5 minutes that you can take out of scrolling mindlessly on your phone, or 5 minutes you take lying in bed a little longer, or 5 minutes you take even just out of your break at work. Meditating stops your mind from racing with all these thoughts all the time and has you just tune into your body and how you're feeling at that moment. I believe we often get so caught up with our own personal obstacles in life that we never have a chance to really just sit and check in with ourselves. That's why I think meditation is so beneficial to us. We are able to take even just 5 minutes out of our day and just sit for and with ourselves. Life gets so hectic it's hard to not always constantly be thinking about what's next or what you have to do next day to day. So just sitting for a moment is so helpful and gives your mind the break that it deserves.

When I struggle with anxiety, meditating in the morning has really helped me reel in that anxiety and feel more grounded and open-minded. I have had close friends and family even tell me I seem more happy and content with my life lately and I told them the reason is Meditation. I personally believe if you know that there is something you can do to benefit you and your life with no negative outcomes and all it can do is help you grow and be better, then why wouldn't you do it?

Starting the day off with meditation primarily helps to get my mindset ready and channeled into what I need to get done that day. The way you begin your day sets the mood for the rest of the day. If you start your day off in a calm, levelheaded manner you will continue the day calm and levelheaded. You will be able to really think things through before you pursue them. Meditating everyday has been the most amazing decision I have made. It often leaves me feeling calm and happy.

FOCUS ON YOUR PERSPECTIVE

It's all about perspective. The way in which you look or feel about something determines if you want to do it or not. If you look at something negatively you will, in turn, think and speak about it negatively as well.

The energy you put into anything is what you get out. If you wake up in the morning frustrated and annoyed to even be getting out of bed and complain about all the things you have to do that day, then what makes you think that you will all of sudden have a good day later? When I say it's all perspective, it's all about how you view a certain situation and the emotional attachment you associate with a certain situation. If you feel you're not a morning person, and you keep telling yourself you're not a morning person, what makes you think you will ever be a morning person if you keep telling yourself that? The more you tell yourself something over and over again the more you begin to believe it. For example: Say you work out 5 days a week. Every day you get ready to workout you are feeling unmotivated, unwilling, and discouraged. You may start making excuses as to why you can't go today or why you need to skip. As a result, you may start telling yourself "Ugh I still have to work out today", or "I really don't have the energy for the gym today". If you keep telling yourself how much you don't want to go to the gym and how tired, low on energy, and busy you are to go, then why in the world would you think one day you would just wake up one day and decide "Wow I'm so excited and pumped for the gym"? That's nearly impossible!

This goes for everything in our lives. Perspective is how we view, feel, and think about every decision we make. Instead of focusing on all the things you HAVE to do in a day, try focusing on all the things you GET to do. I GET to drive my car, I GET to get groceries, I GET to pick up my kids from school. I GET to go to the gym. Your mind is a tool, use it. Trick your mind and shift your perspective until you internally believe it.

PERSEVERANCE

I realized as I continue on this journey to promote motivation that motivation is not just it. It takes a lot to get yourself to do something, especially the things you don't want to do. Its discipline, its mindset, and its perseverance.

If you don't know what perseverance is, it's basically doing something regardless of the delayed gratification, starting it and finishing it. I will admit this is something I struggle with, and I know a lot of other people do too - especially the completing a task part.

I didn't realize I had this issue until I met my ex-boyfriend, Justin. I always had boyfriends who just kind of wanted to please me, but Justin was different. He knew how to address things that we didn't really see eye to eye on in a softer manner.

I remember my lack of perseverance got brought up when I told him how I was going to quit drinking, then went right back to it. Then again spoke about how I was going to quit drinking, then yet again went right back to it. I was just in a debate with myself and vocalized that to him. Justin then communicated to me how I always say I'm going to do something and sometimes don't follow through. I was shocked to be honest. I paused, looked at him with confusion and replied, "What do you mean?" Justin responded hesitantly and smiled, "Well you just always say you want to do all these things, and they usually are great ideas, or ideas to help you or others, but then sometimes you don't follow through. It's not a bad thing, it's just something I think you could work on". I remember at the time I was just completely taken aback. I was really focused on my self-growth and learning about myself and others at this time and hearing how I don't follow through was the biggest mental setback for me because it was hard for me to believe. I kind of set it in the back of my mind and continued with what I was doing because I knew I had really strong qualities and for him to pick one and say I could work on it was not sitting well with me.

A month or two went by and we end up breaking up. I was taking this nutrition in counseling class at the time, and my professor wanted us to take this values assessment survey to assess our strongest and weakest values in our life. When I took it, my strongest value was Gratitude which made me smile, and all the way at the bottom was my weakest value:

Perseverance

"Finishing what one starts; persevering in a course of action in spite of obstacles; "getting it out the door"; taking pleasure in completing tasks."

When I saw that at the end of my survey, my eyes were wide open, and I was shocked into disbelief yet again. This was the universe trying to open my eyes. I sat back and reflected, and realized it was true. I often told myself I was going to do something when I got home and didn't do it or was going to finish something by a certain date and would not. I thought to myself if that's my weakness, then that's the biggest thing holding me back from my goals.

I know that I'm not alone. Everyone can start a task, but most do not finish. I know that I don't want to be like most people and you shouldn't either. While this is so much easier to say than to do when life gets so busy, hectic, tiring, stressful, and time consuming, it can be hard to follow through sometimes. I need to rebuild that trust with myself that I have built with others, when I start something, I need to push myself to finish it. I do not want to slack in this department anymore. It's all about mindset, and how I'm going to grow my mindset, my discipline, and my perseverance in the strongest way possible. Once you do those 3 things, I know you can become unstoppable.

DISCIPLINE

It's important to take note and realize you will not be motivated all the time. That's where discipline comes into play.

Forcing ourselves to push and be better and better every day and to show up day in and day out is discipline. Doing something because you said you would, regardless of the situation or circumstances, is discipline. Setting boundaries and saying "No" when needed because you have other matters to attend to is also a form of discipline.

Discipline is one of the strongest traits you can embody. It's the way you set goals and reach them. It's having the ability to control who and what you let into your life. Discipline is something that can always be worked on, it's something that needs to be practiced over and over again. The biggest form of self-respect you can have is when you are disciplined. You are putting you, your body and mind first above anything else.

You can grow your forms of discipline at your lowest moments. Maybe you were supposed to go to the gym today for example, but you kept pushing it off until later because you had a lot of other tasks to do. Now it's time to go to the gym but you just ate pasta and feel bloated and tired so you decide to wait a little longer, then when you wait an hour longer and realize it's time to go to the gym. You have no other excuses other than the fact you are tired and lazy and you "already did so much today" so you decided you will just go tomorrow. Do you know how many people could relate to that example? SO many people, and many more who won't follow through with it and stay home. They start playing video games, or binge watching their favorite show on Netflix when they could have used that time to go to the gym.

For people who are disciplined, they have days like that too, we all do. But where their story is different is they were supposed to go to the gym today because they said they would. Although they either keep pushing it off until later because they have a lot of other tasks to do, or they knew they had a lot of other tasks to attend to before the day even started, they decide to go to the gym first thing in the morning. Now you don't have to worry about it. They get up, put on their gym wear and head to the gym, because they know deep down they have always regretted skipping the gym, but never regretted going.

CHAPTER

2

HEALTH

When people think of the word "health" they almost always think if their physical health. This is just a reminder that when we are talking about our health I'm talking all aspects of health: Physical, Emotional, Mental, and Spiritual. We need to be aware of all these areas of health because if we are not, then it ends up catching up with us in our day to day being. Making sure we are taking care of our minds and bodies is huge.

Allow me to share an experience I had with an eating disorder and how I have overcome it. I think people all over the world struggle with some form of an eating disorder. Whether it's too much or too little consumption, how they view themselves in the mirror, or how they have developed a relationship with food in general that does not feel pleasant. My hope is you can relate and see things from another perspective that could open your eyes to this subject and help others who have struggled with this same issue.

When I was a freshman in high school, I weighed 150 lbs. I was able to maintain that weight all through high school. That all changed when after graduation I went to Egypt for the first time in 13 years! I think it had to do with the fact that I didn't have access to a gym and was just eating whatever food and sweets I wanted. When I came back, I saw I gained 6 pounds and freaked out.

I got a calorie counting app in hopes that I could lose the extra weight I gained while I was on vacation. I realized a few months later I had clearly messed up my metabolism because I set the calories at 1,600 calories a day. On top of that it was very restrictive, which caused me to binge eat at night. At the same time, I was doing an hour of cardio and not feeding my body any more additional calories, burning up to 600 calories a day and probably eating 1-1200 calories a day in total. Because of this I wasn't having periods. I kept losing a few pounds then gaining the same pounds back. I was struggling still to figure out what was going on with me which was a big stressor in my life right at the time.

Ultimately, I made the decision that I was just going to start weighing myself everyday in the morning to see if I could manage it better. Little did I realize at the time that I had an obsession with the scale. After weighing myself every morning, if the number on the scale was not to my liking it would determine my mood for the rest of the day and what I would eat.

I developed an emotional attachment to the number on the scale without even realizing it. If it was higher than expected I would workout extra that day and eat less. If it was lower, I would feel so proud of myself and eat whatever I wanted because the scale showed I lost a few pounds in a day and I deserved it. I ended up just maintaining my weight for a while doing that, when my overall goal was to lose weight. I kept swinging from one extreme to another. This resulted in me identifying that I had anorexia nervosa, which is the fear of gaining weight and doing things such as working out excessively or fasting/skipping meals to prevent or avoid any weight gain.

It took me a while to realize I even had an emotional attachment not just to the scale but to food and to top it off, as well as my self-esteem. I noticed when the number was higher, I would often look at myself in the mirror with disgust, I would think horrible things about myself such as:

"How could you not be more disciplined?"

"Why would you let this happen?"

"You are literally getting fat"

On the other end of it, if I had lost weight on the scale, it was more like:

"Wow see all that work really pays off"

"Skinny queen"

"You look great"

It was a very toxic relationship, and it was not until my best friend Sarah brought it up to my attention. Sarah works out plenty and she is very disciplined about going to the gym every day. I started to tag along and go with her, and she is one of the big reasons for adapting the discipline I have today.

Sarah had told me that it did not matter what the number was on the scale as long as I was happy about what I saw in the mirror. She sat and patiently had conversations over conversation with me about how muscle weighs more than fat, and how weighing myself everyday was inaccurate. There are many factors that contribute to weight fluctuation, especially for women. If you eat more carbohydrates for dinner your body will hold on to more water. In fact, even if you pushed yourself harder at the gym the night before, your muscles retain more water as well.

Furthermore, if you are a woman and you are about to get your period, your stress levels, if you slept long enough, there are many factors that contribute to weight gain and loss within a matter of a day. So over time I started to realize it was silly of me to use the scale as a reflection of how in shape and happy I was or not. I decided to keep working out, keep eating healthy, and stop using the scale and see if that helped me in any way.

I believe that the whole thing with BMI and weight to height measurements is inaccurate. It's something that has been set as a societal normal or what society deems as a healthy or "ideal" body weight. But who can say what makes you healthy or not? BMI doesn't consider muscle vs. fat. That's why if you took a bodybuilder's BMI, they would show to be overweight/obese and unhealthy.

I think there is more to life than weight. I used to obsess over it so much until I realized that there's a mental aspect that comes into play on health as well. If you are not happy with yourself internally but your BMI is good, then I'm sorry to say you're not healthy. Health and wellbeing is supposed to make you feel good mentally and physically, and if you're a little chubby on the surface but happy internally and don't have any health conditions or concerns then so be it.

Dieting is never the way to go. Small lifestyle changes will help you mentally and physically. I still to this day am working on my self-esteem when it comes to my weight and the fear of gaining weight. I'm actually scared to step on the scale even though I'm extremely happy with how I look in the mirror. I go to the gym 4-6 days a week, go on walks with my mom, go on hikes with friends, and eat fairly healthy about 80-90% of the time. Not because I'm trying to lose weight but because I'm trying to stay where I'm at and build healthy habits. When I have doctor appointments and they ask me to step on the scale I ask if it's okay that I don't. They have always said it was fine as long as I have a general idea of how much I weigh for medication or prescriptions they need to prescribe for the doses.

If you go somewhere where there is a weight limit just even making a joke as "I rather not know", or "do I have to look?" They usually giggle and say you can turn around or close your eyes. You just want to do whatever it is you can to help yourself and not fear the judgment of others, because people will always judge you. They will judge you for sitting doing nothing or going out and doing the most, so wouldn't you rather just be judged for doing the most?

At the end of the day, I am doing something to help me. This is something that is benefiting me, so I could care less if people think it's weird. You need to keep trying, keep finding new things to try to help yourself even if it feels like you have tried everything, you have not. You have tried an copious amount sure, but not everything, because if you tried everything you would not still feel how you feel.

Something that I struggled with a lot was yo-yo dieting. Yo-yo dieting is basically the idea of bouncing back and forth from one diet to another. I think a lot of people can relate when I say some days are harder to be positive than others. I tried not to complain about my body and be so hard on myself but that was harder to do than say. I would bring up to friends or family members that I was struggling internally when it came to my disorder and they would tell me things like "just stop thinking like that", or "are you kidding me you literally look good what is wrong with you" or even start getting frustrated with me like "that's enough Jayla I don't want to hear about this anymore". Of course I wanted to stop thinking that way, and I would have if I could have.

When I was going through that I realized that whenever someone came to me for advice or a cry for help, I was not going to shame them for feeling or thinking that way anymore. I was just going to support them. I was going to be their rock, their comfort, their shoulder to cry on. I made it my mission to find the need to understand and ask how I could help, because that is all I wanted and needed without judgment. I think it is good I felt these emotions because now when I meet up with friends or family and we talk I'm able to just listen and find the need to understand.

I started to try to stop talking about it aloud because I realized it started to make my loved ones feel some sort of way and get frustrated with me. When I look back at it all, it is not like I was heavy either, I was fit but I had a little bit of fat or bloat around my waist that I did not like. I made it a priority to do everything to heal from this constant mental battle of bullying myself because of the scale. It was hard, but I was able to do it.

In the process I had come to the realization that I had a food obsession. I thought about food all the time. Oftentimes if food was involved at an event, it would lead me to not want to go, as well as if there wasn't food, I would not want to go. At that time, I could not even control myself around sweet stuff if I was not on a diet. It was extremely difficult. From calories, too the amount of nutrients, proteins, fats, and carbohydrates, it was exhausting to mentally be thinking about those trapping thoughts all the time. I kept trying to find better ways to cope but, in the moment, I felt like I had this constant desire. Anytime I was anxious, stressed, mad, sad, happy I would resort to constantly wanting food or wanting something to eat or keep my mouth busy.

Honestly, I felt this way anytime I had an overwhelming feeling of any emotion whether it was a positive or negative one. I had been using food as an emotional support to keep me distracted or busy. I think it's something a lot of people experience at least one point in their lives. At the time it did help, but after the fact I wouldn't feel really great about myself, especially if the food I indulged in was not healthy.

What I started to do was when I was having intense cravings, I would imagine how it would feel to indulge in what I was craving. I would imagine how it would feel in the moment consuming it. The minute I thought about how I would feel after the fact I did not want to indulge anymore. Of course, this took some time and practice. What I started to do was try to indulge a little bit, like having half of what I was craving rather than the full thing. This would sometimes trigger that restriction aspect in my head again which would cause me to binge.

My tip to anyone who struggles with eating disorders/ yo-yo dieting is to cut all diets and all restrictions. Focus on fixing your mentality and your relationship with your body and self. You cannot go on a diet until you fix what's going on in your head. When you get to your goal weight, what's going on in your head mentally will still be there. Once you get to your goal weight you more likely than not will not be able to sustain it. You will actually end up overeating and over indulging because in your head "you did it" and "you deserve it". You were disciplined enough, you were strict enough, you went hard enough. However, if you weren't happy doing it, you're not going to be happy after the fact. You need to make sure you're mentally well enough at all times, because even though you could be super fit, if you don't fix the thoughts and self-esteem issues going on in your head, you will never be healthy or happy.

There is one thing about releasing restrictions and dieting you should be aware of. You will probably add a few pounds at the beginning of this freedom release. That is completely normal. You are going to have many cravings, want to eat a ton of foods that you were not able to before, so, you may overindulge. You need to be happy with yourself a couple pounds over or a couple pounds under and understand throughout the whole process that weight will always fluctuate. Once you get to a goal weight you will never stay there forever, you will more than likely bounce up and down the scale a few pounds as you make efforts to maintain your weight, and that is completely normal. Go out, be happy, and don't be hard on yourself. You only have one life to live and focusing on your weight all your life is a waste.

I was listening to a podcast, and it said it helps to identify your triggers and be aware of what those triggers are so you can be more mindful of them and manage them. So, after hearing that I tried to take note of when I had certain cravings and what emotions I was feeling in the moment of those cravings. It took me a while to realize what my triggers were, but I finally realized that I had cravings and urges most when I was feeling anxious. I have a lot of anxiety in general but whenever I start to feel anxious, I want to consume something to keep me busy, even if I'm hungry or not. I believe that what was going in my head was that "I already messed up" so I may as well continue, why wouldn't I? I can start fresh tomorrow without feeling guilty.

I wouldn't say I had a binge eating disorder, but I was on the road to one when I was calorie counting on an app and being super restrictive. I had experienced a few binge eating episodes but not enough to categorize myself as fully having one. Well, I guess that is up to the reader. If you are someone who struggles with an eating disorder or has in the past, me saying that I had one yet only had a couple experiences with it may be triggering for the person who has dealt with an eating disorder for years. We have both gone through an eating disorder, but I really believe the length of time you go through something like that has major effects rather than someone who has dealt with it for 6 months.

I took the time to really acknowledge when I felt the craving to binge. Over time it transferred from a binge eating problem to more of an overindulgence problem. I find that it is the hardest when I'm with people or friends. I started having thoughts such as "What if there isn't food involved?" As well as "And if I'm around with friends then what would we even be doing?" I started to feel that there was no point in events, gatherings, or hang outs if there was no food involved. If there was food involved, I would be excited before the gathering but during the gathering I would get anxious and worry if I was going to be able to control myself around a table full of food. There was a time I did not think I was ever going to be able to unthink how I was thinking, but I did. You can do ANYTHING if you set your mind to it. I mean it... there is so much more to life than just one thing to obsess over. There are so many people, so many components and factors to life. Do not waste your life obsessing over one thing. That doesn't do you any good or bring any value to your life. At the least if you find it hard not to be fixated on one thing, then shift your focus on something that could benefit you. Eating healthier, going to the gym, meditating, learning a skill, painting, running.....the list goes on and on.

If you have an addictive personality and find that you are always fixated or obsessing over something then go ahead and shift your focus to something that can better you and make you stronger mentally, physically, or spiritually. Focus on the good in your life, not the bad. I think that I often think back to simpler times a few years ago when I was so happy with the body I had. I never thought about food the way I do now and was eating in a balanced and intuitive way without all these negative thoughts.

I'm healing, and healing is a process. I will never be how I was years ago with my perspective on food, but I can be better and more aware. It helped me want to learn more about eating disorders, emotional eating, macros, hormones, vitamins and how certain foods have an effect on human health in general, which led me to pursue a minor in health and nutrition. So understanding that you need to go through some things to get to another, some will be good and others will be bad, but take the signs for what they are. Soak it up and expand your knowledge and experiences to help others.

THE FREEDOM OF THE SCALE

Over the summer, I came up with the idea of ditching the scale. Now for many people that is like an impossible suggestion, especially when it comes to young adults whose figure is all they think about. I had been weighing myself every morning and it was just getting exhausting. All I was thinking about was food. I was becoming obsessed and I knew I needed to do something different. This is what I decided to do:

1) I'm going to release any type of food restriction in my mind.

2) I can eat or drink whatever I want in the day but be mindful of portions and sizes.

3) I will work out 5 days a week doing an hour of cardio with resistance training.

4) I will focus on other goals and hobbies to distract myself from the thoughts of food.

5) I will brush my teeth right after dinner or dessert if I want to avoid night time snacking.

I have been doing this for almost two months now and my jeans feel better on my body and my stomach looks slimmer. Now when I think about whether I lost weight or not, I feel GOOD about myself. So why should I obsess? What does a number on the scale say when I eat clean, eat what I want, love how I feel, and enjoy my life? There's no reason for me to. I think even when I'm done traveling this summer I'm going to continue to not weigh myself at all. Weight is known to fluctuate. It will never stay the same. I might just weigh myself at the end of the year and see, but if I keep doing what I'm doing and focusing on my health and working out consistently, I do not need the scale.

FOOD FREEDOM

Food Freedom. It's not talked about enough, but many people struggle with it. Whether it's because they are eating too little to be skinny or eating too much to gain weight or because of food restriction. It's hard to find the perfect amount of food to sustain your physique and eat clean day in and day out. Is it possible? Sure, but it requires an abundance of discipline to sustain. Over time you start to feel like you're constantly chasing something, asking yourself is that even considered a goal anymore? When you're constantly chasing something out of reach, you are becoming more and more mentally exhausted about it.

Furthermore, you may start to feel down. You may start to look in the mirror and talk down to yourself and get frustrated as to why you even look like that. You may even start to progressively eliminate foods you love because you have concluded that you haven't been strict enough. At the end of the day, does it really matter? Truly it doesn't and I'll tell you why. If you're not struggling with obesity and you're not struggling with anorexia, then I say LIVE your life.

It's not fun having anxiety about every event that involves food. It's not fun having to worry about if you're going to be able to control yourself around that dish or dessert that you told yourself you're not allowed to have, but all your other friends are eating it. It's a terrible feeling that overall is not worth it. Did you want to look back and remember that moment as a time where you couldn't eat that slice of cake and had all these overwhelming feelings of anxiety, guilt, frustration, and insecurity? No. You want to look back at this memory and remember eating that slice of cake with your friends and laughing and enjoying yourself without any guilt. Something that helped me was I would tell myself repeatedly that "Weight fluctuates and never stays the same. If you just find a balance in your life, then your weight will find a balance as well."

DIET VS. LIFESTYLE

I'm going to be honest. I don't believe in "going on a diet". I think that is something society has brainwashed us into thinking should be normalized and used to get to an ideal weight. If you're trying to get to an ideal weight you need to partake in a whole lifestyle change. That includes your diet. You can't go on a short-term diet change to get to an ideal weight and expect to go back to your eating habits and think your weight will stay the same, no.

You need to change your lifestyle as a whole while still incorporating the food you love with assistance of portion control and moderation. If you change little things in your daily eating habits, it will show tremendous results. For example, if you get an XXL Diet Coke three times a day every time you pass the gas station on your way to work, on your way back and during lunch break, and love Diet Coke then keep it in your diet. How do we modify this? Simple, start small. Instead of going three times a day try going once, or if that's too much, continue going three times a day but get the next size down, a large. After that week, strive for a medium, then get down to a small. I would say mankind has an addiction to soda, so just reducing any sugary drink down to a small will show great results.

Everybody's body is very different and reacts to different foods and workouts in different ways. That's also another reason I don't think "going on a diet" is healthy or sustainable. Many of these diet programs send you processed "slim" bars, shakes, and low-calorie pastries that have all these processed ingredients and chemicals in them. It's better to just change your lifestyle to eating whole foods. When you're having a craving eat that Reese's Peanut Butter Cup you have been wanting! Don't go and eat something that is labeled "healthier" because in reality you just wanted that Reese's. If you eat something else, in reality you're still going to go eat that Reese's and potentially even more than one or two because you have been so restrictive on your diet.

You need to put into your head your lifestyle change so that you can eat whatever you want. Instead of telling yourself and saying aloud "I can't have that." say "I can eat whatever I want, while being mindful of my portions." A counter thought during a craving would be "Do I really want this?" or am I just hungry? ". Once you check in with yourself after eating a nutritious fulfilling meal, and you're still craving that sweet/salty snack, eat it.

EXPERIMENT WITH YOUR BODY

Like I said previously, we all have our own individual bodies that react differently to foods and workout's than others. If you decide you're trying to switch your lifestyle, experiment! Some bodies need more carbs, whereas other individuals gain inflammation and fatigue from them.

Not to mention everyone has a unique resting metabolic rate, some naturally faster than others. There are ways to change that by exercising more, putting on more muscle, or eating smaller meals throughout the day every 2-3 hours. These are all tips to help speed up metabolism. In spite of that, you will never know that about yourself until you experiment how you feel before, during, and after eating certain foods.

Once you find out which foods are compatible with your body type, you can then work towards having your unique fixed diet that is made for you by you! Yes, you can go to a nutritionist for help on this but remember nobody knows you better than you.

Something that has helped me in this journey is trying mindful eating. After I focused on eating clean, I started to crave eating more clean foods. Typically, the more specific foods you eat, the more you will crave those foods. Once I did this, I started practicing mindful eating. I ate when I was hungry and stopped when I was satisfied.

In practicing mindful eating, I felt freer to eat whatever I wanted, without feeling restricted. I think that when we do tests and experiments on our bodies, we know what's best for our bodies. A good tip to help with this is getting a food journal. Try foods you love as well as foods you have never eaten before. Make a column in your food journal of what it is you're eating and how you felt after. Did you feel energized? Bloated? Tired? The same? It's good to keep track of what foods we consume to our bodies, that way we know which ones to incorporate more of or which ones we should eat in moderation.

This tactic will be especially helpful if you work out. If you find out that one of your favorite foods makes you feel bloated and fatigued, you know that you will not be consuming that food as a pre workout meal. I think it's good to take note of these things so we can help figure out what to eat on days we may not feel our 100%. Another good example is if you are sick, you can look through your food journal to find a meal or snack that will make you feel more energized.

CHAPTER

3

INCORPORATING A WORK-LIFE BALANCE

Work life stress can have a huge impact on overall health and wellbeing. It's really important to work at a job you love, or that helps you grow. I have been working for IHop for 3 years (Now 4 years) and I have loved it up until now. We have been understaffed for a while and I went ahead and stepped up my game to help out as much as I could. The day before Easter we did not have a manager on the floor to help the servers out with any of the problems they may need help with such as discounts, ticket mess ups, and customer modifications. I helped the servers with those things if they needed.

Regardless, I went ahead and spoke to my assistant manager Colton about it. We have been friends for a while, working together for the past three years. We have been through a lot together. I actually used to have a serious crush on him for a while and likewise for him at one point too. But we ended up moving past that and realized that we are very different people and have become really good friends. I went up to him after the shift and told him about how much the staff struggles without a manager on the floor. He asked me how I would feel if I were to be a server crew chief. That is basically a lead server, which means when the manager is unavailable, they go to the lead server for assistance. I basically responded to Colton by saying "Well I mean yea, I have been basically doing it already but just haven't been getting paid for it." Colton responded by saying he would speak to my general manager about it.

The next day I came in, which was Easter day. My general manager Joules was on the cook's line when he called my name. I approached Joules and asked him "What's up?". He then announced out loud for all the other servers to hear, "Jayla, are you delusional or crazy?". I responded "What?". Joules repeated, "Are you delusional or crazy for thinking I would make you a Server Crew, when you don't want to talk to customers when there are problems, or get annoyed when there are too many modifications and..". He went on with more but to be honest I was tuning it out because I was so taken aback on how he just called me delusional and crazy in front of all my coworkers. I tried to respond back to Joules by saying "Why would I do work I'm not getting paid for?" but Joules kept interrupting me. I finally raised my voice sternly and said, "I'm not delusional or crazy, so do not call me that." He responded, "I was joking about that, I apologize, but what makes you think I would promote you when you don't and can't do any of those things?" I stated in frustration, "No that was rude, I do not want to have this conversation with you anymore." He turns to Colton who was cooking on the cook's line next to him and exclaimed, "See this is exactly why!" He was referring to our current argument as the reason why he wouldn't promote me, and he was right.

I was so upset that I ran to the bathroom and quite literally started balling. I was feeling so many emotions such as stress, hurt, embarrassment and overload. I could not believe he would talk to me like that in front of all my coworkers, to humiliate me. In that moment is when I felt this wasn't a joke and that he wasn't joking. I felt that he was taking me for granite and all that I was doing for him. I also felt that he talked down to me because he knew I listened to him and would let him. After calling my work best friend Taylor and calling my mom on my break, I came to the realization that it was time for a new job.

Apart from all that happening on Easter, my family was dealing with things at home as well. My mom and aunt were fighting and that is never good. My Sister Layla made a stupid decision, and I was in the middle of texting her back and forth to help assist and calm her down. I was so stressed and overwhelmed by the fact that my family was struggling that day as well. I knew I had to do something, so I did something a little risky. I texted my mom's best friend, who had been distant for a while, and told her that my mom and aunt were fighting. I asked if she could reach out to her and ask her to hangout. She did and they went out and had the best time together. My mom is such a social person, but she never goes out. I think it's because she wants to be there for my aunt Didi who is more of a homebody. I think it's especially important for my mom to be going out more and being more active to keep her mind busy while she is looking for a job. I think being at home in your thoughts like that during a time of distress is the worst thing you can do to yourself.

Knowing she was already stressed about her job situation and then getting into a huge fight with my aunt, I took it upon myself to help them. I don't plan on telling my mom that I went ahead and reached out to her friend because I wouldn't want it for some reason causing another argument between the two of them. But my intentions were pure, and I just wanted them to take some space and realize that no argument is worth the emotional distress they were accumulating to one another. They need to live their own lives and be able to communicate better in those heated moments.

FINDING BALANCE

When it comes to anything in your life, especially work life, you cannot let it take over you. This comes with anything and everything in life, however I decided to throw this under the work category because it is so crucial.

Much of society works in a job that they do not even enjoy. For you to continuously stay later or pick up extra shifts for whatever reason is foolish. Why would you continue to do something you don't enjoy? Let alone do more of it than you typically would? Let me put this in perspective for you: If you were out to eat with a friend who ordered a salmon dish, and you decided to get it, what if you didn't enjoy it? And what if not only did you not enjoy it, but you had to continue to eat it? There could be multiple reasons why you would choose to continue to eat it, possibly the fear of telling your friend or the server that you do not enjoy the dish, or possibly the fact that you were so hungry and did not want to wait for/ pay for another meal. These reasons are understandable. It's the same with staying at a job you do not enjoy.

Although, if we further the salmon entree example, even after you continue to eat the dish you do not like, you then order another side of salmon, eat it, and then come again to the same restaurant even though you do not like seafood! Now that is absurd! You see the correlation? Why is it that we sit and do things, eat things, attend to things we do not like or enjoy? I will tell you why, it's fear.

Fear of being judged, fear of not being liked, good enough, smart enough, happy enough, secure enough, the list goes on and on. Despite that, when is it going to be enough? You need to stop living the bare minimum and living to please others. Live the life you want to live.

Of course, I understand when it comes to many people's circumstances, "It's easier said than done" to leave a job that you do not like to find one you love. But does it hurt to try? Rather than that being your excuse for the rest of your life and continue to show up to a job day in and day out that consumes you, your life, and happiness away day by day. Does it hurt to try? One of my favorite life quotes is:

"We regret the things we don't do more than the things we do." — Mark Twain.

Do you truly want to look back on your life and see how you did not live to your full potential, and you lived to just get by? No, so start now, start finding your passion, your calling, what it is you truly want to do with your life.

Work should be A PART of your life, not your whole life.

THE VISIT FROM BOB

Today was a crazy day. I'm typing this now straight after work because of the shock that I'm currently feeling. I went in today for work at around 8 am and it was the start of a normal shift. I walked in to seeing that I had the back room. The back room is a separate area of tables in a small room that has probably 8 tables total that are able to be moved and transformed to come together just in case there is a big party. I was not in the mood to have the back room, especially since I just had it last Easter weekend. I saw that one of my coworkers, Brody, was already about to take a family of 7 in there right as I was walking so I asked him, "Hey Brody did you want to just take the backroom today?". "Really!?" He said in excitement. "Yes, I just had it last weekend and I'm just not in the mood today for all the big parties."

"Wow. I mean yea, does that mean you will take my section instead?" "Yea" I replied. He was shocked because he had a lousy section. It's literally the section no one wants because none of the customers want to sit there, and not to mention it's kind of small. "Hell yea! Deal". He replied in disbelief.

After the switch we both started taking tables in our new sections as the rush started to commence. It was my third table of the day when I met him. His name was Bob. I went up to the table and introduced myself. "Hi guys, good morning! My name is Jayla and I'll be taking care of you guys today. Can I start you guys off with something to drink?" I expressed with a grin. He began, "Oh so you're Jayla." "Yes ha-ha" I replied in confusion.

With a big smile back, he replied, "Well I'm Bob and this is my friend Sidney. Now Jayla, let's see if you can help us out. My friend Sidney here has never eaten at an Ihop before in her life. She's out here to visit for a bit and I want to give her a little sample of everything."

29

"What!" I was amazed. "First of all, it's nice to meet you Sidney and Bob, but how have you never eaten at an IHOP before that's crazy." I said, astonished.

Sidney began, "I'm from Pennsylvania and where I live there are no restaurants or coffee shops and businesses everywhere like there is here."

Bob said with curiosity as he flipped through the pages of the menu, "Yes, so Jayla I wanted to get some pancakes can I do that?" "Yes, you can do a stack of five, three, or two." "Okay yes I'll take a stack of two pancakes." He flipped through the pages some more. "I would also like some French toast, let's do the strawberry banana French toast, but can we add blueberries to that?"

"Yes of course you can." I responded with a smile as I was writing down the order on my notepad.

Bob then continued. "Hmm I would also like to order a waffle. Can we add toppings to the waffle? Or actually you have flavored syrups, don't you? We should probably leave it plain because we can put the flavored syrups on the waffle. What flavored syrups do you have?" He questioned as he shifted his gaze from the open menu to me. "Yes, we do. We have strawberry, blueberry, and butter pecan".

"Do you have the original?" "Yes, right there on the table." I pointed at the caddy where the old-fashioned syrup was. "Do you have warm old-fashioned syrup?" "Yes, I can actually take that bottle from you when the food comes out and heat it up for you guys." I said with ease. "Okay yes, and then we will have a side of bacon and sausage as well as a side of fruit. Can we do that too?" He said with a smile and mutual gaze.

"Yes of course, anything to drink?" "Yes, I will take a mango lemonade". He looks up from his menu to Sidney and asks, "Would you like an orange or apple juice?" She says with a chuckle, "No I would like a Dr. Pepper Please". Bob adds, "I will take a coffee also, but Jayla, is there anything on this menu you would absolutely recommend we try?"

I took a pause to think then I began, "I would say you guys did a good job on picking a selection of tasty things but if you have a sweet tooth I would definitely recommend the New York Cheesecake pancakes. They are my favorite pancakes here; you can even get just a side of 1 to try if you would like for just $1.89." I noted with great confidence.

"Yes! Add that to the order so that sounds great, but Jayla let me ask you what do you want to be when you grow up? Are you in school?". "Actually, yes Bob I am, I go to Arizona State University and I'm majoring in Communications. I want to become a professor and teach communications at a college." I explained. "Oh wow, so you want to be a PHD student?" "Yes". "So do you want to do that at ASU? Or go somewhere else?". "Hm, I'm not too sure. I think I would probably stay at ASU." I agreed. "Oh Jayla" He began, "You are going to be so much more than that".

I looked at him confused, took a second and replied "Wait what?" "You are going to be so much more than a professor, your face is so symmetrical, you have nice teeth, you are going to be international". "Oh my gosh, thank you so much". I chuckled. "No seriously, you are going to be a speaker, you are going to speak in a room of thousands of people about the world, about our country." He continued. "Do you believe that Jayla, do you feel that will happen?"

I paused again in disbelief with overwhelming feelings of chills. "Yes, yes I do." "You see Jayla, you are feeling how you are feeling right now because I'm complimenting you on something you already know, you know what I mean? Many people give compliments just to give them. They are not genuine or real. I call those people fluffers. Do you know what a fluffer is Jayla?" He exclaimed. "No, no I don't, what is it?" I giggled, in shock. I just couldn't believe there was a man in here that I was serving that was even saying all these things to me, I was in so much disbelief.

"I call people fluffers who just do and say whatever to get by. They do things to stall or take up space, it's not genuine, it's not true, and it's not real. You know Jayla, a lot of people think you need to be 2x better than the people around you to succeed and get to where you want to be, but it's so far from the truth. Because if you think about it, that is way too hard. Have you seen the men's swimming Olympics? Jayla, the difference between the first and second swimmer is always so close." He raised his hand and put a space between two fingers, about 2 inches. "Two inches Jayla, it's almost impossible to be double the best as your competitors but if you're just 2 percent better in anything you do in life you will succeed."

I replied in amazement. "Wow, I never thought of it that way, that's very true." Still stunned with little to say I exclaimed "You know what Bob, I just got chills, but let me go put your order in and I'll be right back." I said nervously with a smile. I headed to the back to put in the order and realized that what he was saying was so true, everyone is always trying to be so much better than one another but really all it takes is being 2 percent better than others around you and you will succeed.

I eventually came back out with all their food and dropped it out to their table. Bob looked so happy. "Wow look at all this food Sidney, this looks amazing". "Would you like any extra butter?" I questioned. "Oh my gosh, yes how did you know I would ask. You read my mind!" he chortled. I headed to the back, got some butter and came right back to drop it out and Bob continued with our earlier conversation.

"Jayla, I see how you serve, you are already 2% better than the people around you in your job, I see it firsthand." "Aw stop, thank you so much". I giggled. "Jayla you know what, you are going to write a book one day, and you are going to title it the No Fluff Zone. Reason being there is a bare minimum line, and you are always two inches above what is expected in everything you do, there is no fluff."

I gasped, I continued to nod as he spoke and started thinking about how crazy it was that he said I would write a book because I started writing this book a week or two before meeting him. Not only that but the next thing he said I remember thinking I would never forget. "Jayla, sometime down the road you are going to meet someone, now it may not be now, or five years from now or even 10 years from now. But there will be someone who comes up to you and they will say "You know Bob don't you?" You may remember this moment and you may not. But if you do, you will remember that there was someone who came up to you and said that all the things that ended up happening to you happened and that person was me." He continued.

I feel stupid now playing this back in my head and typing it out because I really didn't say too much in the moment because it was a lot to take in. I was experiencing a lot of emotions, and not to mention I was still working and had three other tables to take care of, but there was one thing I knew I needed to ask for sure.

I urged, "Bob, what could make you so sure? Like it's so nice of you to say all these things, and I don't think I have gotten this many compliments from a customer before, but why do you feel so confident in these assumptions you're making of me?" He paused, he made a little smirk and whispered, "I could go on forever about this, but I know you're at work, and you are busy and I don't want to take up too much of your time, but if you want to give me your number I could meet you here at Ihop after your shift, whenever you are off, and talk to you more about it then."

Now typically when an older man asks for your number you decline and think it's weird and creepy. I sense creepy men very well too. I am very aware, but the thing is Bob was not like that. I actually really enjoyed talking to him, he was very genuine and very direct, and he talked with confidence. Without a hesitation I pulled out my notepad, ripped off a piece of paper and wrote down my number. "Yes, I would love that, here you are." I insisted as I set down the piece of paper with my number on it.

"Now Jayla, I'm going to text you and I'll be here at 3pm, but I'm going to check in about 30 minutes prior to the time we are supposed to meet to make sure you are still wanting to. The problem with this generation is you never know when someone reads or sees your text, so I always send a smiley face to show them I saw their message." I laughed, "That's really smart, actually I'm going to start doing that."

Although I didn't really know what he meant by that just because on Iphone you can see usually when someone reads a message, not until I walked away to go print out his check did I see he texted me through my apple watch. "BOB here. C U @ IHOP today @ 3pm, OK?" I messaged back "Yes."

As I walked back over to the table, I set down the check, instantly Bob picked it up "I texted you by the way to confirm our meeting time later." "Yes, I texted back" as I set down some to-go boxes with a grin. "Oh, you did okay, I will see you at 3pm." as he gathered the rest of his pancakes into the boxes and put lids on his to-go syrups. "See you at 3, thank you so much for coming in, have a wonderful day." I announced to Sidney and Bob as I grabbed some of their used dishes out of the way and headed back into the kitchen.

As I was in the kitchen and began refilling some of my syrups from my previous tables I just was in surprise. I kept replaying the conversations we had in my head, or more of what he said to me because I really didn't say much. As I was in the middle of all these thoughts and wiping down the syrup bottles Joules came up to me and said, "Jayla there is a guy here who was sitting at a table you waited on and wants to compliment you in front of me." he exclaimed in annoyance.

I was still very upset with Joules for how he called me delusional and crazy in front of my coworkers and has not said sorry. I heard from another coworker that he has no intention of even saying sorry. So, because he has no intention to say sorry, I had no intention to say any extra words to him than what was needed. I didn't even respond, I just followed him right back out to the lobby from the kitchen and there was Bob. He exclaimed with confidence, "Joules, Jayla here is an excellent server, and you should promote her to some sort of trainer or something." Joules recalled "Yes she actually is a trainer." "Well Joules,

Jayla was the best server I have had in my life. If any of your staff was anywhere near as good of a server as Jayla is here, you would have a really great thing going on here."

As Bob continued to talk to Joules, I couldn't help but wonder what Joules thought about his gesture. Bob ended up leaving after his conversation with Joules. Joules and I were walking into the kitchen together Joules said, "You know the compliments he gave you were nice and all but he could of saved the words and just gave you 50 bucks." he recalled in the most snarky voice. I walked over to Bob's previous table to bus it as well as pick up Bob's signed receipt. He literally tipped me 50 bucks. I went up to Joules and announced in excitement, "Oh my gosh he literally tipped me 50 bucks as well." "Oh wow, great job" he uttered. I walked away and continued to attend to the other tables I had to cater for. All I kept thinking about is this was no coincidence - God is sending me a sign.

As my workday came to an end I got a call from Bob during my shift at around 2:30pm to confirm our meeting. I missed the call but walked away somewhere private in the back and let him know I was still up for our meeting. I thought I would be done with all my side work and cleaning, but I wasn't, so I asked my assistant manager Sully if it was okay if I clocked out on break while Bob came in to talk to me. "Who is Bob?" he looked at me with confusion and itched his head. I explained to him how I think he is some sort of medium or psychic. I really needed to talk to him, and that I would clock out on break while I speak to him and the minute I was done I would clock back on and continue my work. He seemed unsure but I think he saw how eager I was and agreed to it.

Eventually Bob arrived. I saw him on the camera in the back, so I walked up and told him to follow me, and I walked us to a booth, and we sat down.

He began as he interlaced his fingers between one another over the table. "Jayla, you asked me earlier how I knew what I knew, and how I was so sure of the statements I was making. You said you were from

Egypt so is it fair to assume you are Muslim? And believe in God?"
"Yes, I am and yes I do." I responded with confidence and a smile.

"Okay, so you may or not believe this, but I have a guardian angel and
so do you. When I saw you, it was my guardian angel that was telling
me to tell you all the things I was saying to you. There was so much
it was telling me to tell you Jayla." I just sat there making eye contact
with Bob as he continued. I was so fascinated, I really did believe the
things he was expressing. I felt close to Bob as if I knew him before, I
felt comfortable, it was weird because I never felt the way I was feeling
before.

Bob carried on with genuine eye contact and a compassionate tone, "I
believe Jayla, me and you knew each other in another life, a past life,
we knew each other. I think I was supposed to meet you here today and
I think you were supposed to be my server. If not here, we would have
ran into each other somewhere else today."

As he continued, I started to think about how crazy that actually is.
Earlier today the section I had wasn't even supposed to be my section,
it was Brody's. Even before it was Brody's, it was originally supposed to
be one of my other coworker's section named Felma. But Felma ended
up being the expo for the day (which is someone who pulls and preps
the food after the cook's finish cooking it). So, Felma gave the section
to Brody so she could be expo', Brody switched his section with me so
he could have the backroom, and I ended up having that section for me
to meet Bob. It was really hypothetical.

Out of the blue, I watch a roach crawl on Bob's shoulder. "Oh my gosh,
oh my gosh, Bob there's a bug on your shoulder!" I spoke frantically as I
was fanning my hands in shock. "Oh just flick it off for me, would you?"
he suggested in the most calm manner. I hesitated for a second, took a
deep breath then just flicked it off. I didn't want to touch it because it
was a roach, but I also still knew he was a customer and didn't want him
thinking we had bugs because we absolutely didn't. We have never had
bugs let alone a roach. I could not believe I had just touched it. I tried

to play it off and continue with our conversation, but under the table I was tapping my feet up and down constantly because of the fear that it would crawl up my pants.

A few minutes went by when all of a sudden, the bug climbed up again but on the other shoulder. I was going to ignore it and not say anything in hopes he wouldn't notice but I just couldn't not say anything. "OH MY the bug is literally back on your other shoulder!" I blurted out in distress as I flicked it off again. "What kind of bug was it? A fly? A Gnat? Mosquito?" he questioned in curiosity. "It was a literal roach. I'm so sorry we don't have bugs, I don't know why it was crawling on you." I confessed with hesitation. "Oh wow, well let's move over to that booth over there since this one has some sort of infestation." he chuckled.

We moved over to another booth by a window with much more room and sat across from each other. I elaborated to Bob about my situation here at Ihop and how ironic it was he asked to speak to a supervisor and told Joules in front of me how he should promote me. I also told Bob about how I had 3 interviews on Monday. He asked me where they were, and I told him: The Nook, Original Chop Shop, and Cheesecake Factory.

"You know it's good for you to get a new job Jayla. I think it's time. That's no way a manager should talk to you. If anything, this job is holding you back. Joules is cancerous to you, it's time to leave. Now you would make good money at the Cheesecake Factory, but you would have to work nights, and you don't want to work nights huh?" He inquired. "Yea I should leave, it's harder to do than say because I have been here three and a half years. I basically grew up here, but yea I would not like working nights at all." I acknowledged as I put my elbows on the table and interlocked my fingers and set my head on top of them.

"Well, it would also interfere with your schooling, so you don't want that. Now the Chop shop, you wouldn't be serving, or making as much money as you do now. The Nook is a breakfast place, right?" he added. "Yea it's not a serving job but they serve healthy food and I love that, and yes The Nook is a breakfast place and instead of being open 24 hours like here at IHOP it's only open from 6 AM to 2 PM." I explained as I tucked my messy hair behind my ears. "Ah so The Nook is your best bet. You would like it there; you would work mornings, and you still be able to serve which is something you're experienced in."

"You're right I would be happy there, hm I guess we will see how it goes. I will let you know how the interview goes. I think my thing is Bob is I don't like change, I freak out, I don't like the thought of the unknown." I spoke unsurely. "But Jayla, everything in life is unknown, everything you do every day is not set in stone. It's up to you, life is changed." He assured me.

I was nervous, I didn't want to leave IHOP, but I knew I had to. I didn't want to go to interviews, but I knew I had to. I mean it's fair, I hadn't had an interview since I was 17. All these thoughts were running through my head, like what if they don't like me, or I'm not good enough, but Bob definitely gave me that push that change is okay.

"Now Jayla I know you said you didn't have much time to talk but I did want to just say I know when you tell your parents or friends about this interaction, they would think it's weird, and I understand that. So, this could possibly be the last time we see each other and that's okay, but I want you to watch the Inventor and text me once you do and if you have any questions about it." he added as he stood up out of the booth and motioned his hand outward towards me with a fist.

"Yes, I will, thank you again so much for your kind words, you really made my day." As I giggled, I motioned my fisted hand out towards Bob as well to give him a fist bump. I walked back to the kitchen to clock back in then headed to the dish pit where Sully was washing dishes. As I began to sort silverware so I could run it through the wash Sully set in a rack of dishes and closed the dishwasher. He turned towards me as he was taking off his dirty gloves. "So how did it go with that guy out there?" he questioned as he smirked with a little giggle.

I didn't really want to go into depth about it, but of course I did. When something great, abnormal or unusual happens in life and you tell people around you about it they usually tend to downplay it and say that whatever strange thing happened to you is untrue. Since my story involves someone who is a lot older than me they may say something like he's crazy or it's bull and I didn't want my perspective on what just happened to be reconstructed.

As I set down the tray of dishes and began sorting out the forks into my divided bin, I took a deep breath and looked at Sully with an unsure expression "It went well, but there was a roach that crawled on him twice. I had to flick off." Sully raised his eyebrows with a shocked expression on his face, "What really, was he upset?" "No, he wasn't, but the first time the roach came on his shoulder he didn't even know, I just told him it was a bug and I flicked it off. But when it came the second time he asked what bug it was and I told him it was a roach, so we moved to another table. It didn't seem to bother him much at all, but it was weird because we don't have bugs." I explained as I moved on to sorting the knives.

Sully paused for a moment, as if he came to some sort of realization that he was processing in his head, "You know Jayla, they say that certain animals and insects have some sort of spiritual meaning, have you tried searching up what a roach landing on someone's shoulder means?" "What really? I did not know that! Let me look." I took off my gloves and tossed them into the trash right next to me and pulled my phone out of my apron and began to search. "Oh wow, it says that a roach landing on someone's shoulder signifies a major change, rebirth, or transition in your life." I affirmed. "See I told you! Now that's crazy." he chuckled with an interested look on his face. "That is crazy, see what I mean, I can't believe this is even happening to be honest." I said with great shock.

Bob and I stayed in touch here and there. We called a few times, he came to visit others, and we kind of just drifted apart from talking as much, which was fine to me. I knew life was getting busy and I'm sure he was too. He stated this would happen and that if we ended up not talking as much it would be okay. He just seriously believes I am and will be something great, and honestly, him coming into IHOP is all it took. He is and was the start to everything.

As I've been writing this book I have come to many realizations. One big thing being that everything really does happen for a reason, I have become far more spiritual because of it. I notice when I'm at certain places and run into people I believe it was for a reason. When I drop something, I believe it's a sign to slow down, or if I find a hair in my food I believe it's because I'm not supposed to eat it. When we become more aware of the grand scheme of things and all the people who flow in and out of our lives, it helps us to be able to take control of our lives and navigate it better. I will forever be thankful for Bob. If we ever speak again or not, he was one of those people that crossed paths into my life that truly made a difference for me.

FRESH START

The day has come. I left IHOP and started at the Nook on May 1st. I might say I love it. It used to be run by the same owners of First Watch, which is another brunch place, but they split off and have their own franchise. It is so different from IHOP. I am about to start my third day of training tomorrow and the staff is so friendly. They are a little strict, which is fine, just not what I'm used to. They do not let you have your phones out during your shift at all because they are always wanting you to be busy. They do not have a heat lamp for the food when it's up, the cooks yell "Hands" and you as a server, even if it's your table or not, are required to go grab the food and send it out to the table.

They also have paper tickets that print out for the cooks once you send an order in, very old school but I love it. The girls that work there keep talking about how good I'm doing, which makes me happy because I was so nervous to start working there for the fear of not doing well. But I'm catching on quickly and they can see that. They let people who are in training get a free meal at the end of their shift. I think you get 50% off when you are off of training, but I've been getting their sandwiches that are heated like paninis with a side of mixed greens. I bring it home to split with my mom while we watch Love After Lockup, it is such a vibe.

THE NOOK VS. IHOP

I actually ended up leaving the Nook. After a long first shift off training, I was unhappy. Not only did they ask me to be last on and vacuum the whole dining room once all the servers and tables were gone, I also had to give a percentage of my tips to the hosts and bussers. While I understand that's very normal at a lot of restaurants, I was not used to that at all. I'm used to just busting my own tables and keeping the 30 bucks.

So what did I do? I called Joules. He picked up of course. I expressed why I was upset and he understood and apologized and told me he was purely joking with me and it wasn't right to joke about. I really did appreciate it because Joules never EVER apologies. Which means he really meant it. I of course accepted his apology, and he put me back on the schedule right away with my usual 5 am shifts. Some people could see it as a bad thing that I went back, but my efficiency skyrocketed. I was #1 server ranked, my beverage sales were high, I had really high sales, and I was excited to go back to work.

I'm happy that I left for The Nook, but I'm also happy I came back to IHOP. Leaving showed me that I'm just really grateful to be back at IHOP and I know I am good at my job there. Not only did it help me appreciate it, but I think it made Joules appreciate me more too. After a week of me being back at IHOP he promoted me to a certified trainer of the store. I was so happy, and he even gave me a little pin (He knows I love my work pins). Sometimes time apart from whatever it is in your life gives you a chance to be without it, reflect, and miss it or move on. In this case I missed it.

This will always come with trying new things. There's always going to be the alternating feelings between if you like it and want to continue

41

with it. In this case the Nook was not for me, which is fine, because it made me value, thrive, and respect my job more than ever, and most importantly, I'm happy.

I have been at IHOP for about 4 and ½ years, (not counting the week I left to the Nook). I love it there, Joules and I have gotten much closer, the whole staff I love very much, and the environment is just so fun and lighthearted. I really do enjoy going to work there. I truly believe that people should work where they love, where it makes them happy. I think if you continue to be a hard worker at something you love you will eventually move up in that department and flourish at your work.

It really sucks that society has normalized how we work a 9-5 job that is mediocre, or often we hate, go home, eat dinner, watch TV, go to sleep and start the same day over again. Then on the weekend go out and spend a couple hundred dollars at the bars or clubs. I just know that's not the life I want to live, and you shouldn't either. Do not let anyone dictate your life and who you want to be. When that ends up happening you will end up being in a job, profession, or circumstance you hate because you were trying to please other people.

Stop pleasing other people, and please yourself. At the end of the day people will judge you regardless of the decisions you make and what you do, so just do what you want and what you love.

CHAPTER

4

LIFE LESSONS LEARNED

"Everyone who enters your life comes for a reason, some stay for a few paragraphs, others a few pages, and some a few chapters." Unknown

I believe that everyone who comes into your life is brought into it to teach you something. I picked out a few people that I had met along my journey and added them into this book. I changed their names so that they won't know it's them, I mean I hope they don't. But if they do, I will try to leave out too much of their wrong doings... I don't know, I guess we'll see. I want to share this because I am a firm believer that we learn the most from experiences and conversations with others.

If you really think about it, all that we are taught in school and learned is from events, conversations and experiences from other people. It is all about what they have learned from going through what they have, and they share it with others. So going through and meeting the people I have met, I have learned a great deal. What I'm going to share with you, you may find that you have gone through a similar scenario and came to a realization the minute I share what I learned or noticed. My goal is to open your eyes to every relationship in your life and how it has an effect on who you are and what you do from that point on after the knowledge you gain from your involvement with that individual.

ROLAND

So, a little back story, I dated this guy almost two years ago and he was so handsome, literally tan skin, green eyes, fit, masculine and so romantic. I was so into him. We were talking for a while and probably dated almost a month. It doesn't seem like a lot of time at all now that I say it but we talked for a good amount of time. Anyways, we ended up breaking up. He broke up with me because he was moving to another city that was almost 2 hours away and told me he doesn't know if he could keep up with the relationship.

I was so devastated because I really wanted it to work, and I've wanted him ever since. We had each other blocked but not until recently as in a few days ago I received an Instagram dm and snapchats from him. He was basically saying how much he missed me, and he's sorry he hasn't texted me sooner but he didn't know how to from how things ended.

I sent him my number and told him to call me, and he did. When he called, he restated what he said over text and told me he has had enough time to date around and talk to other people and he just kept thinking about me. He also said he works a lot in my city and keeps driving past my neighborhood, or the park where he asked me out. He told me that all he thinks about now is me and he wants me. I told him that's nice and all, but I would like him to tell me that when he's sober. He said he would, and I ended the phone call. He told me he would talk to me tomorrow.

This is how or text conversation went down:

Roland- "Hey"

Me- "hi"

Roland- "What's Wrong?"

Me- "Nothing's wrong I'm just thinking about what you said last night"

Roland- "What did I say?"

Me- "What do you mean? You said how you missed me, can't stop thinking about me and want to be with me."

Roland- "I wasn't blacked out Jayla, I do miss you and I know you don't want to waste your time and I don't either. I know we have both changed so I want to hang and get to know you again and see where it goes from here."

Me- "Yes I completely agree."

Since those messages we have had a few phone calls and texts, but they weren't very in depth. I did ask him to send me a picture of what he looks like now because it has been like two years and saw that his hair grew out long and he has beard, which I don't really like. I guess we will see how it goes tomorrow when we hang out for the first time. I'm super nervous, I hope he doesn't cancel. I just really need to see him and see if this is truly what I want.

After hanging out with Roland, I realized it wasn't all that I was hoping and expecting for. I had been hooked on Roland since we broke up a year ago and wanted him back so bad because of the pure fact that I couldn't sit with the fact I was truly being rejected. I had never truly experienced firsthand rejection until I met Roland, and I think that's what made me so intrigued because he was something I knew I could not have. But then when I saw him (he was even better looking than before), I knew it wasn't what I wanted and seeing and speaking with him reassured that. I was happy I got to see him, because I think it gave me the closure I needed to let go and move on. As we know, rejection can damage our self-esteem and self-worth (Winch, 2013).

When I saw Roland, he complimented me on how good I looked, and I quote "Wow Jayla you got pretty, like you were pretty before, but you're so much prettier now". He also noticed my efforts from the gym since I've seen him such as "Wow Jayla, you got abs!" He noticed other positive changes about me such as "You have changed" and I replied "I have. But how so? In a good or bad way?" Roland responded as he had one hand on the wheel and stared across at me with his beautiful green eyes, "You have changed for the better, you're more mature and calmer." I feel once I saw for myself how he wasn't what I wanted and how he reassured me it had nothing to do with me "not being good enough" I was ready to let go.

Roland taught me that often we want what we can't have. Furthermore, because of my limited access to him it made me want him more. Not thinking about anything else but just wanting him. Not the red flags, not the negative times, not our differences or even communication issues. All I knew was that I wanted him. This caused a big page turn in my life because we often get blinded by everything else when we are so fixed and focused on something we want, and feel we can't reach or have, that it starts to affect us mentally. Feelings such as you're not good enough, or "What's wrong with me". But that's not the case at all, rejection is okay, rejection helps us learn why something didn't work and to find another way or person to make it work and apply different tactics the next time around.

TAMMY

Where do I begin with Tammy? Growing up working at IHOP I met Tammy. We worked together and he's a few years younger than me. He ended up becoming my gay best friend. The phrase "I would do anything for you" was essentially who Tammy was to me. Tammy would do anything and everything for me if I let him.

Tammy and I stopped being friends once the whole time we have been friends, and it was for a year. I got overwhelmed by him constantly wanting to hangout and if I said no or wanted to go home early, he would get mad at me. So, I slowly tried backing away from him. He noticed and did not like it. He confronted me about it, as he should, and I told him that I was overwhelmed and needed some space.

He did not handle that well at all and quite literally said it's just better we are not friends anymore. I told him if that's what he wanted then fine. After the fact he started posting these crazy videos all over social media screaming to breakup songs, saying how selfish I was, how I wasn't a good friend, how we only wanted to do what I wanted to do. I was very hurt by the videos that all my friends, coworkers, and some family members saw.

Tammy was someone I trusted, and I was extremely hurt. A year or so went by and one of our close friends Bliss passed away. It was devastating. We went to the funeral and my friend group as well as some of my friends from work went out to lunch after the funeral and had a little party to celebrate Bliss. I invited Tammy, and that was one of the best decisions I have made in my life.

We were there for each other, we hung out more and more, talking about what happened in the past and how we hurt each other and where our communication was lacking. I told Tammy that he hurt me and that I'm willing to be friends again. He understood and was willing to be friends again even knowing it would probably never go back to how it was.

As time passed, I was right, our friendship never went back to how it was. In fact, it was better than ever before. Our communication was stronger, our trust was built, and our support for each other was unlike any other. Tammy eventually moved out of his mom's house, lived on his own, working two jobs, barely getting any sleep, living paycheck to paycheck and his family did not
speak to him. Tammy has gone through more than any person I know, especially at his age, yet
has been the best friend to me I have ever had in my life.

He has hit rock bottom so many times in our friendship, yet still was an amazing friend. He always found a way to get to me if I was not okay or if I needed him. He knew how to push me and calm me down in ways no one else could. Always. The days I was down or insecure, nope that was not an option when I was around Tammy. He knew the minute I was not okay and pushed me to talk it out and to discover why I was feeling the way I was.

Tammy has taught me it is okay to not stay friends or in contact with people you love. It doesn't mean you won't be friends ever again, sometimes the comeback after the storm is what makes the bond stronger and more invincible than it was before. I think after cutting contact we both had time to sit and reflect on what went wrong, where it went wrong, as well as where we went wrong.

So, when the time comes where you cross paths again, you have had time to process, calm down and analyze what happened as a whole. Then you can communicate and apologize where it is due and talk about concerns you had. I'm so happy Tammy and I are friends again and I'm so happy we stopped being friends, because we would not be the people nor have the friendship that we are and have today.

CLARA

Clara, she is one of a kind. Many people may perceive her as "Alot" or "Too Much". She has a big personality, talkative, emotional and a little sensitive. I met Clara when I was a freshman in high school, and she was a Senior taking a theater class as an easy last elective. We hit it off, but when she graduated, we were not really in touch anymore.

Later, we got back in touch, and all was good until COVID hit. I was going through a brutal breakup at the time, and her uncle just passed from COVID. I felt all my friends were there for me except Clara. I tried communicating that with her then, but it started to become a battle of whose situation was the worst. We stopped being friends because we were not seeing eye to eye or were there for each other.

A year passed by, and we reconnected and met for coffee to talk. We tried to elaborate on our feelings at the time and why we were frustrated with one another, yet we still did not seem to fully agree, but we agreed to try our friendship out again. Clara was always one to talk. She talked so much that sometimes I would cut her off or not giving her the time of day to talk because it was too long, and I really just wanted her to get to the point.

Just as I talked about previously, when our friend group found out that Bliss passed away it was one of the hardest things I have experienced in my life. Although it changed my friendship with Clara forever. The minute I found out and called the group chat about Bliss passing, Clara dropped everything and drove to my house to support me.

I was bawling and crying in her arms. I was telling her that it feels like there is anxiety in my heart and she explained to me it is grief. She checked up on me day in and day out, calling me, trying to get me to get out of the house. Even though she was hurting, she was trying to be strong to help me.

As days passed, I looked at her one day and we locked eyes. I started tearing up as I told her with sympathy, "I am so sorry I was not there for you when your uncle passed away. I was so selfish. I was so caught up in my breakup that I had no idea what you felt or what you were going though until I felt this with Bliss. This feeling of grief I have now that Bliss is gone is like my heart is aching. I couldn't imagine how you felt when you lost your uncle, and for that I'm truly sorry".

She looked at me and gave me the biggest bear hug. She was there, and she heard me, she listened to me. The thing is, she will probably never forgive me for how I treated her when her uncle passed away and I would not hold it against her to hold bitterness towards me because of that. But the way she was able to look pass that and be there for me when I was mourning speaks volumes on her character.

Clara has taught me to feel for others. I've always seen her as so sensitive, but she taught me that society as a whole has become insensitive. Everyone is in their own world, focused on themselves, worried about fitting in or what people think, but not Clara. She always stood out; she was always unapologetically herself. She communicated when she was

49

upset, hurt, or frustrated. She danced, cheered, screamed, and laughed when she was happy. She is Clara.

Clara has taught me to be patient and taught me to seek to understand, before seeking to be understood. Sometimes you don't know what the other person is going through or what they have had going on that day. When you seek to understand, it can shift your perspective on the situation, and you can respond according to the details you have gathered.

Society in general wants to be heard, wants to be right. In reality, we are all just talking over one another. There is barely any common ground when it comes to anything. We are the same but different, and not the same because we share the same materialistic items and follow the most popular trends. We are the same because we all just want to feel valued, loved, heard, and understood.

BLAKE

After taking some time to focus on myself after Roland, I went ahead and continued swiping left and right on Bumble (a dating app). I came across Blake's profile, and we eventually matched. We exchanged socials such as Snapchat and Instagram.

There was a time, I'm not going to lie, when I was talking to a few guys at once and would often find myself leaving Blake on delivery for days. But there was something that stood out about Blake. The way he complimented me and would have conversations in such a way where he seemed to share genuine interest in me. Instead of just texting back and forth over Snapchat, we started replying with video responses to one another. It made me feel really comfortable really fast to want to actually meet him.

The one thing I find that is a struggle for me, even though I'm so extroverted, is when guys show an interest in me and want to meet up. I have no idea why it stresses me out. Maybe it's because of the chance of them being weird or me possibly not being able to go home when I want to. I find myself often standing guys up, or canceling at the last minute which is terrible but it's really me not them. Anyways, after multiple conversations with Blake and getting to know one another, I had shared with him my love language which is words of affirmation and gifts.

One Saturday morning I was at work, and he asked me what my favorite drink from Starbucks was if I had to pick. I texted him back that brown sugar oat milk shaken espresso is my all-time favorite. A few minutes went by, and he texted me that he was outside. I was genuinely in shock and ran out the back door to see him sitting in his car. I had the biggest smile on my face and exclaimed in excitement "Hi, oh my gosh!" As he handed me the drink and a pastry in the Starbucks bag, he mirrored my smile on his face with engaging eye contact and said, "Hi so nice to meet you finally! I got you a cake pop too, do you like cake pops?" Blake questioned. "Yes, I do actually!" I paused while holding eye contact sipping my coffee in front of him and continuing, "Mmm so good, are you going to get out and give me a hug or what?" He chuckled and began, "Of course I am, I'm coming into eat as well, are you going to be serving me?" He replied flirtatiously.

From that point on began me and Blake. He would come into Ihop all the time and we got close very fast. He met all my friends and even my mom. He saw me probably 6 days out of the week if not 7. He almost seemed like he was the perfect match for me. Always so patient, never got upset or talked to me in a rude manner or tone. He truly was one of the most genuine people I met.

He had these very deep brown eyes, probably 5 '11 or 6 feet. He had a well-kept short beard and looked a little like Taylor Lautner when he was younger and in Twilight, but with longer hair on the top and cut shorter in a fade on the sides. Everything seemed perfect, especially after he met my mom. However, days passed after Blake met my mom and he still hadn't asked me out.

I brought it up to him and the first time he told me it was because he wanted to make it special and didn't want it to be cheesy for him to ask me out right after my mom approved of him. He then went into depth about how he would ask me out right now if I wanted him too. I told him no, I understood, and I did want it to be special. After that conversation a few more days went by and we went to get acai bowls at Melissa, my best friend's place of work. She asked us why we haven't started dating yet, and he started saying something different than what he told me a few days prior. He told me that he wanted to wait until after I got back from Mexico and Egypt and that it wouldn't make sense if we had started dating and I was traveling all summer. When Melissa walked away to help a customer order, we continued the conversation and I agreed with him. He elaborated and reassured me he wouldn't be talking to anyone else and that he would purely be working on bettering himself.

A few weeks had gone by and one of my favorite people came into Ihop to visit me around the same time Blake came to visit me. It was Bob! I sat him down at a table that was far from where Blake was because I had a rotating section that morning. Because Blake had come in earlier, I was breaking a different server at a different section than I was when Bob had come in. I was a little busy upon Bob's arrival so I took his order and told him I would be back to chat. He got his usual, two over medium eggs, a large side of salsa, and four strips of bacon. He ate this with a hot cup of coffee, of course. Once I caught up on all my tables I returned to chat with Bob. He had asked me about Blake, and how the two of us were doing.

I chuckled, "We are really good Bob, he's actually right over there." I pointed across the restaurant to Blake where he was sitting, already staring over at me talking to Bob with a huge grin on his face. Bob stood up from his seat, stuck his hand up and waved. Blake mirrored back his wave as he was sipping a cup of coffee. Bob sat back down and said, "Should I go over there and talk to him?" I responded with shock and excitement "Wait really? Yes, oh my gosh, he would love that!" Bob smiled and spoke calmly "Does Blake find our relationship weird? What did he say when you first told him about me?"

I responded in confidence, "Honestly no not at all, he has not told me that he thought it was weird or unusual at all. I'm sure it looks like that, but I have talked to highly of you and he thinks you express really great care for me, so he has not said anything negative about you or said otherwise." Bob held the grin, "Should I go over there or have him come over here?" I smiled and he knew, Bob began to stand. I gathered his silverware and coffee, and we walked over to Blake's table.

Once Bob introduced himself to Blake and got settled, I refilled their coffees and left them alone to talk and get to know each other. I knew at this point in time I had feelings for Blake, but I also had some reservations, as did my mother. However, after my mom met him, she definitely saw why I was so drawn to him.

He was just such a wholesome person and very genuine, his intentions were so pure, and it was clear all he wanted was the best for me. I was very excited for Bob to talk and get to know Blake. I knew that Bob also wanted the best for me, and he would speak truthfully and honestly not just to me, but to Blake as well. Once their interaction together was over and Bob left, I asked Blake what he thought of him.

Blake took a deep breath and spoke casually, "He is a really cool guy who definitely has a lot of knowledge. I told him about how I wanted to be a professional golfer and he gave me a number to a friend of his that I can reach out to. He could possibly help me and get started on the right path to getting to where I want to be." "Aww that's great Blake! That is so kind of him". I exclaimed with joy.

Eventually Blake left IHop and when I went to check my phone, I saw Bob texted me to call him after work so he could enlighten me on his thoughts about Blake. Once I got home, I was very excited to call Bob because at this point, I had really valued his opinion. Bob shocked me a little at first. He basically told me Blake is a great guy and cares for me a lot and would treat me like a princess, but his goals are very hard to reach. I had asked him to elaborate.

"Blakes job right now is just purely for survival, which is fine, he is young, but that is not what you want. Blake told me he wants to be a professional golfer, which is a nice goal, but only 1-2% of people really make it to professional golfing, and you must be really good. Now, not saying he wouldn't be able to do it, I'm sure if he's very good it shouldn't be a problem. But let's say he does become a professional golfer, and you had a family with him. He would be traveling a lot and would hardly be home, is that something you would be okay with?"

At that moment I realized what Bob was saying. Blake is such an amazing guy, like probably one of the most genuine guys I have ever met. But Bob was right, this was not what I wanted either. I would be fine being a stay at home wife but the fact of the matter is I don't want to be raising kids purely on my own and be away from my significant other all the time. Bob had told me that he predicts I will call him a month from now and we will go from there.

After that conversation with Bob on the phone, I continued to think about what he had told me, and I tried to imagine my life in the future if I stayed with Blake. I didn't think we would be a good match, so I ended up breaking it off. What made it worse was when I texted Blake explaining how I felt and how I was overwhelmed and just didn't think we would be a good fit because we were at two different spots in our lives, he was very understanding.

That was something I was definitely not used to. He actually heard me out and respected my decision. He did text me a few times after that asking if we could meet up and talk once more before I headed to Egypt. I did meet up with him and it was not a good idea. I think he could agree with that statement as well, and I will just be leaving it at that.

Blake taught me that it's okay to try new things and get out of my comfort zone. He was different than other guys I dated because he didn't just do whatever I wanted to do. I mean sometimes of course he did, but if I wanted to go to Starbucks for example he would say "No how about we try something new?" and we would. We went hiking together on NEW trails, grabbed coffee at NEW coffee shops, ate out at NEW restaurants. He was always pushing me to try new things and it made me feel more comfortable overall with the idea of change.

Even though Blake and I do not keep in contact at all anymore, there is no bad turmoil. He has helped me break out of my shell more than he knows. I am always pushing myself subconsciously, even if it's the smallest change like parking in a different parking spot at my gym or switching the way I make my daily coffee every once in a while, or just hanging with new people and doing new things.

I do still get anxiety right before trying something new and I am working on it. I think I worry about the unknown and the possible outcome. That's what has always kept me doing the same things and going to the same places because not only is it comfortable, but it's predictable. So, I am still pushing myself daily to try new things, holding myself accountable to it and not letting anyone enable me.

JUSTIN

After Blake I started to get a crush on this guy I worked with named Justin. If I'm being honest, I liked him before talking to Blake, but once I ended things with Blake I had this desire to try again with Justin. I couldn't tell you why I liked him so much, but his confidence really intrigued me, and I wanted to know more about him.

The issue with Justin though is that he doesn't want to be anything because we work together. I am totally okay with that because that could go south so quickly. The other thing about Justin is that he kind of has a gambling addiction. He doesn't think so, he said he could stop whenever he wanted it, but I don't really know. Anyways one morning I came in at 5 AM and he was finishing up his shift as the overnight server. He told me he was going to go gamble right after his shift at the casino, and I began, "You know, I'm actually good luck right." I spoke in confidence, batting my eyes at him. "Oh, is that so? Well then if that's the case." He reached over to one of the ticket printers and held down the button so it could print out some paper and he ripped off a piece and handed it over to me with a pen. "Why don't you go ahead and write me a note then for good luck?" He replied flirtatiously with a grin. "You know what I will do." I folded the piece of paper and simply wrote...

You will Do Great.

And you will WIN!!

Goodluck :) - Jayla Embaby <3

I handed it back to Justin "Here you go". He took the paper, folded it up and put it in his pocket, "Thanks, I'll update you and let you know how it goes."

After my shift I went to go workout at the gym, and he still hadn't texted me. It had me second guessing about my note. I know it was weird, but it wasn't that I was even just trying to impress the guy. I had this strong feeling that he needed some sort of hope or luck. A few hours later I get a text from Justin:

I forgot you don't have snapchat, but thanks for the Goodluck I went up $1500

When he sent me that text, I knew there was something special in me I had to learn more about. It wasn't a coincidence either, because since this time he has won multiple times more since holding my note with him in his pocket. The times he didn't keep or have the note I gave him he, lost money drastically. I think that there is something about believing and manifesting not just for you, but for others. The fact I wrote a note basically affirming he will win and that I believed in him must have triggered some hope and belief that he would in fact win, especially if he had read my note over and over a few times before going to the casino. Hearing or reading something over and over will cause you to eventually believe it.

A few weeks had passed, and Justin basically told me he didn't want anything serious. I was really upset because I had felt that he just wasted my time, so I communicated that with him. When I did, he basically replied "Jayla you knew I didn't want anything serious." I replied to him explaining how if he didn't want anything serious then why did he ask if I was talking to other people, or wondering why I'm upset, or when he figured out why I was upset why did he try to change his actions to make me happy if he didn't want anything serious?

I was really upset and told him to leave me alone he replied, "You got it". I was furious, I didn't know how to calm down. I applied the 5-minute rule (I'll go into detail about this later) and then did my 20-minute meditation before bed. I decided to follow up with a better text considering I know he overthinks heavily. I simply said "Listen, don't worry about it, don't overthink. There aren't any issues between us. I hope you have a goodnight and I'll see you tomorrow at work". I thought this text would show that I can handle my emotions and be a bigger person, but he solidified that he was a smaller person when he left my text on read and didn't show up to work.

I obviously still don't know why he didn't show up to work the next day. I know he had personal family issues, but he was not good at communicating with me at all, which is hard when my love language is gifts and words of affirmations. When the next weekend swung around, and we were both working the Saturday morning shift, we flirted on and off like nothing had ever happened. He rolled my silverware for me Saturday, then Sunday asked me if I could help him, so I did.

He texted me "hey beautiful" later that day, we snapchatted back and forth. We were keeping a steady conversation up until I asked him "Wanna hang out Thursday?" He left me to read, so I in that moment realized his intention and efforts were not aligned with mine. I responded with "okay" and he then started typing in the chat. I simply blocked him, and that was that...until I work with him this weekend of course.

It's funny because I had typed this part of my book months ago but now, I'm back editing it because I ended up flirting with him on and off throughout the shift. I told him I'm not playing these games anymore and if he wants any chance with me, this is the time because I'm not doing this anymore. After that conversation with Justin, he completely switched. We went out to froyo, we got dinner, he hung out with my friends, and I hung out with just him. We went to diner after diner all around town having coffee and pancakes with strawberries and whip cream, my favorite, and we would talk about our lives for hours and time just flew by.

We realized we had so many similarities that we have never had with anyone else. We kept going out, he was such a gentleman, opened all my doors, paid for me date after date, and talked to me in such a kind soft tone. Never raised his voice at me, was so patient. So, we started dating. We are still dating now and he's amazing and has taught me so much.

One of the biggest things he taught me is that there really is not a right or wrong view of the world or a particular situation. I feel I was always very closed minded growing up, and if people did not view things how I viewed it they were essentially wrong or selfish. Although talking with Justin about life and our upbringings, I recognized I was so far from the truth.

He would ask me a question on my beliefs on a particular topic and I would then explain and he would acknowledge what I said. He would say something such as "Yea that makes sense" or "That's a good point I never thought of it that way" or "Wow yea I can see that for sure". He would affirm that my views and beliefs were validated and understood why I viewed something the way I did.

In spite of the fact that he did not always agree with me, he affirmed that he heard me and then began his reason for believing what he believed without putting out that I was wrong, and he was right. He was able to acknowledge that my view was right as well as his. We had two different upbringings, two different backgrounds, and two different experiences as well as grew up in a world as a man and a woman. Yet, we were still able to find common ground and conclude we were both right in our beliefs and perspectives on the topics we were discussing.

That was beautiful to me, I had never met someone who was able to share their beliefs with me without dominating the conversation and pointing out the reasons why I was wrong. It was so refreshing; he was just such an amazing human that needed to be protected at all costs.

THE 5-MINUTE RULE

What is the 5-minute rule you ask? Well, the 5-minute rule is basically a strategy to use when you get angry or upset. When an event takes place, and it happens to affect you negatively, apply the 5-minute rule. Set a timer, and you can cry, scream, throw, punch, whatever it is that you usually do to release stress or frustration. Once the 5 minute timer is over you simply release whatever your feeling to the universe and you don't let it determine the mood for your day. If you let it stay in, it's just going to shadow the negative feelings throughout your whole day. And that is not what we want. Applying this rule may seem tricky at first, but after one or two tries you will be amazed at how effective it is and how much better you will feel at not having the weight of holding onto a grudge on your shoulders.

JUST DO IT

Something else I have learned and implemented is the idea of "Just do it". As we all know it is the famous Nike slogan, but it has helped me tremendously when I'm stuck on my phone, or I really want to get something done and I feel I just cannot.

We are all human. We have moments where we feel drained, worn out, or out of energy essentially. I believe when we are feeling that way it's when we need to push ourselves the most.

For example whenever I check my phone and feel I get stuck mindlessly scrolling on it video after video when I have so many things I need to do I will ultimately just stop, count out loud " 1.. 2.. 3..." and just drop my phone and essentially "Just do it." I count out loud to initiate the thought that this is happening, and this is happening right now. Not in a bit, not later, not tomorrow, no, right now.

DEDICATIONS FROM DISTRACTIONS

It's important that if we have goals, we want to achieve that we are able to separate the distractions from the tractions. Being able to sit and watch a show should be okay, but not every day for hours. Society has made it culturally accepting to binge watch our favorite shows on Netflix for hours while sitting on the couch with a bag of chips. More so than not, that show you're watching isn't doing you any good or bringing you any form of physical, mental, or emotional value.

Technology is a blessing but also a curse. It is amazing in various ways of connecting us with loved ones who live far away, more efficient ways of scheduling, booking, and setting up meetings, as well as being able to stay up to date with all your loved one's lives via social media. Social media is also very time consuming and has an addictive aspect to it. I don't necessarily think it's a bad thing if you know how to control it in moderation. It's normal and human to want to just sit down and not think and just destress from time to time, but because of the feeling we get from the dopamine being released to our brains during this mindless scrolling in them becomes addictive. Our brains love the feeling of being stimulated, especially with little to no effort needing to be made.

Once you are able to acknowledge the time that goes by when you are in one of these distracting episodes, then you are able to make small changes to help quit it. Something that helped me is realizing how long I've been on my phone and how much of that time I could have used to better myself mentally, physically or emotionally. Some examples include working out, reading, journaling, or mediating, or doing some face to face interactions such as spending time with friends/family. If you learn to shift your mindset from just relaxing whenever to stimulate your brain, to actually doing something to stimulate your brain and working towards it, it feels much more fulfilling. Here is an example, being tired and going to the gym. Once the workout is complete you feel more energized, pleased, strong, happy and more fulfilled then when you started. You got that bit of the happy hormone, which goes by the name of Endorphins.

CHAPTER

5

BREAKING OLD HABITS

Oh Habits, are habits a good or bad thing? Habits are typically something that is done repeatedly subconsciously because we have done it so many times our mind and body just effortlessly do it without thinking about it. I decided to pick out some habits I want to break and record and analyze how I felt after it.

I'm going to record and make notes for 14 days straight, breaking a habit. I'm going to go into detail about changes I felt from my body, thoughts, triggers, things that have helped me overcome and push through the temptation of the habit, and just basically the good, bad, and ugly of it all. I have quite a few habits I would like to break. I sectioned some bad habits out I decided to experiment with so if you struggle with that habit as well maybe reading my experience may help you break it and taking some of the tricks I had incorporated into consideration when you're ready to break that habit yourself.

NIGHT SNACKING

I decided to go ahead and try to get out of the habit of night snacking. I'm going to journal my nights and how difficult it was and hopefully this could possibly help you if this is something the night that could possibly cost hundreds and hundreds of calories. If I want a dessert, I'm going to have it right after my dinner and then go brush my teeth. I'm journaling to hold myself accountable and this is how it went.

Day 1-

Not hard at all, I had a 1/2 of a Whataburger cookie that I split with my friend after dinner and brushed my teeth. I felt really good about myself when I woke up this morning and didn't have any cravings for the rest of the night.

Day 2-

Honestly it wasn't too bad, but I did get a craving and pushed through it. I don't want to necessarily restrict unhealthy foods or sweets, but I do at night because I have come to the realization there's no way I can take just "one bite" - it causes me to spiral. So, I'm hoping that on Day 2, I found one of my triggers.

Day 3-

This night was the first night I did not snack while having friends over. At first, I started to feel anxious because I'm usually a casual eater when I'm around people. When I got home after getting Açaí bowls with a friend, I had a few graham crackers and a bite of dark chocolate, then brushed my teeth and threw in my retainer. The thing is, I actually went ahead and took out my retainer later in the night and had a protein powder peanut butter ball I had made for my YouTube channel. I felt like it did not cause a trigger to eat or have more, which was shocking because I have identified that snacking at night is one of my triggers. I feel that I successfully went through day 3 strong, let's see how day 4 goes!

Day 4-

I ended up having a late dinner this evening at 8:30, followed by a snack of peanut butter protein powder on a rice cake. I mixed water in the protein powder, so it was easy to spread. I wasn't too happy about eating that it made me anxious. Even though it really was not a lot of food or a big snack I think I have identified another one of my triggers.

- New Trigger Unlocked: Eating anything too late at night. It makes me really anxious and want to pursue emotional eating to cope.

Day 5-

Day 5 honestly was not bad at all. I ate out a lot earlier in the day, then went to the gym late at night and got home at like 9. After realizing how not eating late at night has made my body overall feel better before bed, and in the morning that almost over took the temptation and I did not feel the need to snack at all. I did want to eat a little something that had protein though because I did hit the gym, so I ate a peanut butter protein ball and brushed my teeth and went to bed.

Note: One thing I would like to note is I've noticed snacking at night comes from not eating enough in the day or restricting yourself too much during the day. I have started telling myself instead of "I'm so hungry" or "I wish I could have this and eat that", I have started telling myself "I can eat whatever I want if I want it" as well as "I'm not even that hungry, but If I want it I can have it". There is something about knowing you're able to have and eat whatever you want that makes you not want it as bad.

Day 6-

Day 6 was my friend Alice's 22nd birthday so I went to a gathering. I chewed on some gum when I was feeling anxious at the gathering, and when I got home it was easy for me to not even head to the kitchen. I went straight to bed.

Day 7-

Really easy wasn't even thinking/ craving a night snack at all tonight to be honest.

Day 8-

I was nervous I was going to crave food, but I had a Chipotle bowl right after the gym, so I felt satisfied. After that I went to IHOP with Tammy to do some personal work brushed my teeth and put on my retainer before we went and just got right to work. I didn't get a craving, however I did get anxious of the uncertainty behind the possible thoughts of getting late night cravings.

- New Trigger Unlocked: Feelings of anxiousness, any type of uncertainty, and lack of comfort.

Note: Making sure I eat enough throughout the day and at every meal.

Day 9-

Night Snacking was a little harder tonight because there was a change in routine. My aunt came home from Egypt tonight and because I was already feeling anxious all day today and her being home and us sitting and talking in the kitchen then living room and her handing me some of her airplane snacks was hard but I had my retainer in, so it was easy for me to pass up.

- New Trigger: When I start to feel anxious.

Day 10-

Was not bad at all, I went out to dinner with friends then got coffee. When I got back home the craving for a night snack was not even really a thought in my head.

Note: Having a pack of gum, once done eating/ drinking something out of a cup such as a wine glass or red solo cup, a cup that's open, at social gatherings or popping in a piece of gum right after helps me from feeling anxious or cravings.

Day 11-

Today was hard because I went out to eat at an unhealthy restaurant and kind of ate a lot at the restaurant, or at least I think I did. When I got home, I had some more of my leftovers because I was craving it. But once I ate some, the cravings went away.

Note: not labeling food as good/bad, removing restrictions from "bad" food. If you're hungry eat it, if you're craving it, have some. I also noticed days I don't get enough sleep, my food cravings are all over the place as well, so I need to start prioritizing sleep.

Day 12-

Tonight was the first night I went without brushing my teeth and putting my retainer in right after dinner. I went out to Ihop to see my friend Tammy at work. I wanted to see him before I left for Egypt. I just had a few cups of coffee and made sure to have gum on hand if I had cravings. I didn't have cravings, I enjoyed the coffee, and chewed a few pieces of gum. I'm very proud of myself.

Day 13-

I ate dinner tonight and had no cravings naturally. I didn't even have to put my retainer on to help myself. Things are getting easier, and I'm getting a hold of my temptations and cravings at night.

Day 14-

I did not need my retainer. I had thoughts of eating something else, but no urge or cravings. I knew that if I ate really late, I wouldn't feel the best in the morning so that made me aware of my body's signals towards how it feels eating too late at night.

Post Experiment Reflection-

After this experiment I realized that just a few days after the recorded 14-day mark, I had no urge, temptations, or thoughts of late-night snacking. I think one of the things that got me to overcome this habit is telling myself I'm allowed to eat whatever I want if I'm still craving it in the morning or during the next day. If I still wanted it when I woke up the next day then I would end up eating it, but I usually wasn't. This experiment also made me realize one of my triggers is late at night. I can't just have a bite or two of something sweet and then stop, it would trigger me to want to eat more. But if I had the same sweet treat in the daytime, I could take a bite or two and stop. There's just something about eating late at night that has a different effect on my willpower. I'm happy I did this experiment because I was able to identify some of my triggers, ways to avoid them, and work with them to prevent them from happening.

WAKING UP FIRST THING IN THE MORNING AND USING MY PHONE

Another Habit I decided to work on and break is when I wake up every morning, the minute my alarm goes off, I go on my phone. Some days it's just for 10 minutes, others at 30 and others it's an hour. But any amount of time on your phone right when you wake up is terrible for you. This is a habit I've been wanting to break for a while, but it was really hard to even get started. I was wanting to start this like a week ago but kept caving in. I finally was able to start it and this is how it went.

Day 1-

I had set my alarm the night before for 8:30 am, but I did not wake up to my alarm. I knew since this was the first day of me not using my phone right when I wake up, it would be stupid of me to grab my phone to just "Look at the time". There would be no way I was going to be able to have enough self-discipline to not read notifications, messages, and scroll on social media.

Knowing that, an amazing idea popped into my head. With my tired and raspy morning voice I asked, "Hey Siri what time is it?" Siri replied back, "It's 5:54 am" I was in shock. I had never woken up this early naturally, so I went back to bed.

When I woke up, I sat there for a while without my phone, just staring at the ceiling. I was feeling anxious. It took me 10 minutes before I got out of bed and because I do not have a clock in my room, I decided to make my bed and head downstairs to look at the time. It was 7:36 am. I began my day by doing something around the house for at least 20 minutes before checking my phone. I felt like I had more energy and was definitely more motivated to take on the day.

Day 2-

I thought day two would be easier, but it definitely wasn't. Let me start off by saying I was trying to call out for Siri to ask her what time it was about 10 times with no response. This instantly made me irritable, which then made me anxious. I was tempted to just go on my phone. I tried to curb the temptation by thinking about my plan for the day.

I then found myself constantly having my thoughts go back to reasons why I should check my phone such as "I need to check to see if I got paid" or "I need to text my friend happy birthday" "I need to see how many likes I got on that Instagram post from the night before and respond to the comments, so people don't think I'm ignoring them". It was crazy how tempting it was this morning. Another thing I noticed when I was staring at the wall again this morning after waking up was that my eyes vision was blurry or fuzzy. It could just have been because I just woke up, but I didn't have that day one which makes me wonder if it has anything to do with the blue UV rays that my eyes have adapted and getting used to in the morning since every morning for the past 9 years I have gone on my phone when I woke up. I'm curious now, I guess we will see how day 3 goes.

Day 3-

Today I had to wake up at 3:30 am for work, so I kept pressing snooze. I accidentally hit something half-tired to see a notification and read a text and it affected my mood more than usual for the worse. Usually, I start the day off late without my phone and with a clear mindset focusing on what's in front of me. However, because I saw that notification, it's all I was thinking about until I got to work.

Day 4-

I woke up and checked my messages quickly again by accident. It was my cousin and she stressed me out, so I had to call her at 4 am. I started my day off stressed. I'm going to try to turn off the alarm and get up on my own tomorrow.

Day 5-

This morning, I simply turned off my alarm and got up. It was easy to do, but I started feeling anxious in the morning and thinking "What if" statements. I was wondering if I would be missing out on an important text or email. I made it my goal to wait until I got to work to really look at my messages, and once I did there was none.

> Note: it was 5 in the morning after all, so I think knowing that there were no messages all along helped my anxiety and knowing that I'll check it eventually; it doesn't have to be right then and there.

Day 6-

I cannot tell you how good I felt today to wake up before my alarm and not worry about a thing. I also didn't feel as groggy as I usually do when I'm checking and on my phone. I felt so at peace, content, and ready to start my day.

Day 7-

I woke up before my alarm once again, but I just sat there. It's hard trying to get out of bed when I'm not on my phone reading or watching things to wake me up. I kind of just stare at the wall or toss and turn and fall back asleep. It has helped me feel more in tune with my thoughts and self, but I still feel anxious.

Day 8-

I meditated outside today when I woke up before work and was taking my dog Mini out to pee. I'm really enjoying waking up without a phone in the morning. It has cleared my head and I am able to think about what I'm going to be doing for the rest of the day without those racing thoughts of anxiety.

Day 9-

I woke up without the thought of checking my phone this morning. I hopped out of bed ready to start my day.

Day 10-

Layla woke me up today to braid her hair before school. I had no urge to check or go on my phone. As a matter of fact, I took my dog out to pee, I went to the bathroom, brushed my teeth, washed my face, braided her hair and then I checked my phone. It's so relaxing not waking up to checking my phone first thing in the morning.

Day 11-

I checked my phone just for the time and got up to start getting ready for my day.

Day 12-

I had no urge to check my phone other than for the time. I put in my head that after I brush my teeth and do my meditation/journaling, I can check my phone and respond to texts.

> Note: Putting in my head that I am allowed to check my phone after I wake up and complete my morning routine, rather than putting in my head I'm not allowed to check my phone at all. Telling yourself that you are allowed rather than unallowed to do something will help release the urge of temptation.

Day 13-

Easy, woke up with no urge.

Day 14-

Woke up tired but no urge to check my phone further than checking the time.

Post Experiment reflection:

After focusing just 14 days solely on breaking my morning phone usage, I realized a lot about myself and how after staying committed and disciplined, I was able to overcome this bad habit that I had thought I would never be able to break. My phone usage first thing in the morning every morning was one of my worst habits. I learned that if I could overcome this habit I could overcome any of my bad habits by just staying committed, disciplined, and consistent.

ADDICTIONS

Oftentimes when we have a habit, its main root is because of an addiction we have. For example, I decided to quit night snacking, could the possibility be because I had an addiction to food? Well, I would say yes. I was previously on a very restrictive diet which had led me to not being able to enjoy the foods, sweets, pastries, and drinks that I love for a long time.

I was always constantly thinking about food and waiting for my next "cheat" meal. Eventually my cheat meals became cheat days, which lead to binging. I would binge so much and eat so quickly that the next day I would work out so extremely or restrict my calories so much and even incorporate fasting some days to compensate for all the stuff I had eaten the day prior.

That was not the way to go. I had to stop weighing myself and look in the mirror and tell myself I am happy with who I am and how I look right now, and not restrict myself anymore. I continued to eat healthy, and have the pastry, drinks, and sweets I love, but I learned to do it in moderation. When you tell yourself you can do or get whatever it is you are craving if you wanted to whenever you wanted to, it relieves some tension off of the fact it's "bad" for us or on a limited supply. It's hard to break something we are addicted to, especially when it has become something we are so dependent on.

I try to analyze things I do every day and decipher if it's a habit or addiction. Once I figure out if it's a habit or addiction I decide if it's a "good" or "bad" action. If it's good I move on to the next, and if it's bad, I remove the connotation from my head that its bad and try to focus on why I'm thinking it's bad by asking myself these questions:

1. Does it distract me from my goals?
2. Does it cause me harm or make me sad, angry, or anxious?
3. Does it suck the energy out of me or make me feel lazy?

Once I ask myself these questions, I figure out what I can do to change or limit these actions. For example, when my alarm used to ring in the morning, I would snooze it a few times then go on my phone and start answering texts or scrolling through my newsfeed. If we applied this to the 3 steps above this is how I would have responded.

1. Does it distract me from my goals? Yes, sometimes I find myself scrolling on social media for 30 minutes to an hour. I just keep telling myself "One more video". Before I know, it I just blew hours away when I could have used that time to do something productive.
2. Does it cause me harm or make me sad, angry, or anxious? Yes, it makes me feel all of those things. I start to obsess over why someone is active on social media and not texting me back and get angry. Or I get sad because I see my friends went somewhere without me and didn't even shoot me an invite text to join them, or anxious when I'm away from my phone.
3. Does it suck the energy out of me or make me feel lazy? Yes, I feel like I could just sit there all day and stare at my phone. It makes me tired and want to sleep after I'm done even though I didn't do anything physical but move my thumbs to scroll or text. I feel if I stay on it for a while I start to get a headache, or my eyes get sore.

Once I reflected on this, I make it a priority to not look at my phone straight out of bed. I should at least go ahead and make my bed, use the restroom, brush my teeth and wash my face, and then I can look at my phone. But even then, I try to do it standing up so I can make it a quick check rather than get stuck scrolling on a social media platform for hours.

I noticed that in the first few days to a week of breaking this habit, I had become really anxious. That was hard to cope with just because it made grabbing my phone more tempting. Since I was already feeling that anxious feeling, I started to base my thoughts off of that anxious feeling as well such as "What if someone is urgently trying to contact me" or "What if that cute guy texted me and I'm taking too long to respond, and he becomes uninterested" or "What if my mom is trying to reach me and gets mad its taking too long". These thoughts stormed through my head all at once, which made no sense to needing to be on my phone urgently when I was up at 7 AM and most of those people were probably still asleep anyways. I really tried to push those thoughts out every time they popped up and tried to make sense of them.

SECOND CHANCES

Do you believe in second chances? Well, you should!

I never really used to believe in second chances, in fact I used to hold extreme grudges over people and cut them out of my life completely. Until I realized that life is all about messing up, learning, and growing. Just like you are meant to meet people as lessons, you are a lesson for them as well, whether it be because they messed up or you were the one that messed up. I think everyone interprets these kinds of scenarios differently, but I do believe that we are meant to love and forgive.

The biggest thing I think that causes people to be hesitant about second chances is they are scared the same situation will play out again. It is up to you if you are willing to take that risk. Life is all about risks, every decision we make in life is a risk, and it is all about how you go about the outcomes of the risk you choose.

For many people I don't think they change right away, it seems to be more gradual. I think this is because as humans we hate change, maybe even a little terrified of change. We are creatures of habit and routine because we know it is what is safe and what works.

Back to what I said about change being more gradual. Sometimes we change not because we want to, but because we must. For example, many people change after a loved one passes. They have to be strong; they may change the ways they act, talk, or even their outlook on life. The hardships we experience throughout our lives make us more grateful and happier after we have finished pushing through that hardship.

It's hard to realize something like that when you are going through a hard time. When we are going through a rough patch or hard time, we can feel like we are falling into a deep hole and unable to get out. When you're in that deep dark hole, you are alone, you feel trapped, there is no way out. Once you're out of that hole, you will most likely reflect and look back at the hole. You will feel accomplished. You got out of that hole when you never thought you would.

You will realize how you grew on your journey out of that hole. Now being in the hole in the first place did suck, but now you know how to never fall back into that hole again because of the actions that lead you to be there in the first place. You know now you will want to avoid that hole, because you learned. You will never be in that position again, or if you are, you know how to get out because you have done it before.

Many people do this with relationships. They go through a tough break-up, feel alone, isolated, hurt, betrayed. Then once they have had time apart, they think that the no-contact rule break did the trick and get right back together again. This is not an accurate way of handling a situation because over time you will fall right back in that hole and be hurt yet again. Now with enough time to do this, you will eventually not want to let people that close to you again, you won't want to be vulnerable because in your head you "tried so many times". But you didn't. You tried one time, and saw it didn't work, climbed out and fell right back into the same hole over and over again. You are so hurt that you are scared to ever let anyone else back in, so you isolate yourself.

As podcast host Mindset Mentor Rob Dial stated, "In order to see change you must have inspiration or desperation". Referring to something positive and inspiring, or something negative and distressing. Something inspiring may be your past challenges and struggles, your family or friends, ambitions, charities, etc. Some examples of desperation include loss in family, financially, physically, or emotionally. When you feel you hit rock bottom and there is no other option but to get better and be better and grow.

BEING COMFORTABLE IS CONFINING

When I tell you that being uncomfortable was something I really struggled with, it was. I felt safe in comfortability and routine. I loved going to the same food and coffee shops and ordering the same drinks because it's what I knew. It's what I liked, and I knew it was safe and secure, and that made me feel good.

I have been this way my whole life. I don't know if it's because I grew up an only child and my mom always reminded me time and time again to be aware of my surroundings and be safe, or anything new that seemed the slightness bit risky she was against because she would think the worst of any risky situation. I think I followed that mindset right after her and always kept it in my head subconsciously. I need to be safe and make safe decisions, so I stayed in comfort.

As time went on and I became more driven, I was really focused on my self-growth and expanding my knowledge to the public. I wanted to be a motivational mindset innovator/speaker. I felt like I kept posting the same things having the same routine week after week time and time again with little to know growth and I didn't understand why. It wasn't until I realized, I'm too comfortable.

I began to do more research on success and growth of individuals, and realized I need to put myself in uncomfortable situations. Being uncomfortable is the key to growth. When we are stressed, uncomfortable, overwhelmed and go through hardships is when we learn the most the minute we get out of it.

We put stress on our minds/bodies to be able to navigate the situation and know how to get out of it if the situation occurs again in the future. Or if we have a friend, family member or loved one who goes through a similar scenario, we can help guide them. It's hard to get uncomfortable, and don't I know it. It can be so anxiety-inducing. It's almost like all the what-if scenarios just start racing through your head uncontrollably.

When we can determine that we are in-control of our thoughts and that our feelings strive from our thoughts, we are better able to control them. We can switch negative thoughts for positive ones or even neutral ones. If you are telling yourself "I hate how my hair looks today," then start trying to tell yourself "I love how my hair looks today", that's ineffective.

It's ineffective because you are trying to give yourself a thought that you don't even believe in yourself. That's when it's nice to switch from negative thoughts to neutral thoughts, such as "I have hair". That's a neutral statement that we believe because we do. So being able to just notice those moments where our thoughts drift off and become negative to reel them in, push it out and implement neutral thoughts that will be very effective for you.

When it comes to being uncomfortable, start with small things, such as:

- Parking in a different parking spot than you would usually.
- Ordering a different menu item than you typically would.
- Hanging out with a new friend or family member you haven't seen before or haven't seen in a while.
- Trying a new coffee spot.
- Push yourself to do something when you are feeling extra nervous about it.

When you push yourself past that fear or stress and get through it, you will in return grow from it. Keep pushing yourself, especially when it feels intimidating.

STOP GIVING PEOPLE POWER

Stop giving people power over you. If you really think about it, this is a habit within itself. We subconsciously get used to pleasing people or letting them have control of our emotions to the point of it getting too far and too out of hand to stop.

When we give people power to have control over us whether that be control over what we do, our emotions, thoughts, actions, it continues. That's why it's important to never let someone have that control. If they think they are, or can, you put your foot down to it right away. In certain relationships that become abusive, it almost seems shocking to the couple because it progressed right under their nose. One day they wake up and are shocked sitting and wondering how this even happened, and when it even got to this point.

It's the little things. Everything in life is the little things. It always starts off small and progressively builds up. The minute you give someone leeway or leverage to have any type of control over you it will escalate. That's why it's so hard for some people to leave harmful relationships, because often they realize how much control they have gave this individual and try to restructure and take their power back and then that makes it worse.

When we give people power it can make us feel unfit, indecisive, insecure, self-conscious, stupid, and dependent. People who have control over us make it hard for us to make decisions in our day-to-day life without consent or validation from the person we gave power to. If we go ahead and restructure the power into a more positive outlook, we can see how their words can also be uplifting, such as when they complement us. That then makes us feel good and superior but when it's stripped of us, or they do not compliment us, we may start to feel insecure about how we look or question why they didn't compliment us.

If we give people power for how we feel, then we will always need constant validation from people. We do not need any validation from anyone but ourselves. You need to be YOUR number 1 fan and #1 supporter. If you can't be there for yourself, you can't be there for others.

CHAPTER

6

THE LITTLE THINGS

The day of March 30th did not start off too bad. I got up and weighed myself. It wasn't the worst but also wasn't the best. I had two classes that day I had to attend and had already gone to my first class of the day. My professor for my upcoming class said that attendance was not required for class today, but I wanted to go because we had to pick an artifact that resembled a reason for why our last relationship ended.

I chose this black bear stuffed animal and key chains from this diner in my city that went by the name of "Black Bear Diner". I loved and still love that diner to this day. My ex- boyfriend, Milo, was struggling with drug addiction, and every time he messed up or lied to me about it, I would freak out and get upset. Milo knew my love language was gifts and words of affirmation, and although he did both really well, his words of affirmations were not as strong anymore because of all the broken promises. I didn't believe his words anymore. He would get me gifts, or take me to Starbucks, or take me to Black Bear Diner, or the mall. He really did everything he could to make me happy whenever he could, and I'll forever remember that and appreciate that.

The Black bear and key chains were a gift he got me for Valentine's Day, and I was not happy with it at the time. Because I feel loved and valued by gifts, I see gifts as a way people notice the little things about you, remember small things, and when they purchase a gift, they they know you will love, you know how they truly think of you. When I asked him why he got me a keychain and a bear from Black Bear Diner for Valentine's Day, he said because I like the restaurant and he thought I would like it. Of course, yes, I like Black Bear Diner but that doesn't mean I want my whole Valentine's Day gift to be Black Bear Diner themed.

It took time for me to realize it was more than just a gift, it was a symbol. A symbol portraying all our memories at Black Bear Diner as we went a few times a week. We were always happy at that diner no matter how bad the fight was prior; it was always a happy memory when we were eating there. It represented why I stayed for so long because he knew how to make me feel loved, regardless of the struggles in the relationship. His intentions were pure in giving me that gift, but I did not realize the thought of it until months later.

That is also when I realized there are only so many gifts you can give someone before they realize that you can't really buy happiness if you don't have a sustainable happy relationship. Those gifts made me temporarily happy, but when his words didn't match up with his actions over and over with countless broken promises, over time it just isn't even worth it anymore. One can be just as hurt and in a relationship with someone you don't trust.

I think it's important to reflect on the little things in your life, especially in a time of frustration, anger or depression. We often get so caught up in our own head that we don't appreciate all the little things that made our day enjoyable. It's hard for me some days to just stop and be in the present moment. I'm always focused on the next task, object, or event. It is especially hard for me to just stop, breathe and take in everything around me. The noises, the temperature, the sounds, the people around me, the vibes, and just being present in the moment. You only have one life, and all these little components and moments are what make up the big picture.

I was unhappy at the time Milo got me the stuff from Black Bear Diner as a gift and I was ungrateful at the moment because I was expecting something more traditional, like flowers, chocolates, or a necklace. However, when I reflect back to that memory, I see he did so much more than that. He had his own struggles just like everyone else, and decided to choose something that was of great value to our relationship. He chose something that symbolized the heart and happiness of our relationship, somewhere that we were both at peace in the eye of the storm of craziness we were going through together. It's ludicrous that it took me all this time to be out of the relationship and reflect back now to realize that and appreciate it.

Whenever we are caught up in our own head, we aren't focused on anything we are grateful for or appreciate. We are focused on *"Why did that happen" "I can't believe this" "This always happens."* We are focusing on "why are things happening to me" when in reality the mindset should be, things are happening for you, not to you. We need to prioritize our happiness above all, but how do we do this? We'll reflect back on a day when it was just the best. When you were happy; when it was fun; the vibes were uplifting and light.

Things to Consider:

- Who was there with you that day? Was it a friend? Multiple friends? Perhaps maybe even family members, or maybe a mixture of both?
- Once you think of the day that made you feel cheerful, think about what you did that day.
- Did you go to your favorite local coffee shop?
- Cook your favorite dish at home?
- Go bike riding around the city?
- Go on a walk?
- Did you listen to your favorite music artist while going on a drive?

Once you list off everything from that favorable day that made it truly amazing, then reflect and try to incorporate some of those aspects in that day to your everyday life, at least 1-3 of them. Whether it was cooking at home, seeing your family, or grabbing a coffee at your local coffee shop. Incorporate as many feelings as you can into your day to make everyday a blessed, happy, and positive day. It will make your day a little bit better by uplifting your mood, which will change your mindset for the rest of your day to a joyful positive one. Which will result in another happy day.

It's the little things that come together to make up the biggest outcomes. Many people believe you must have a boring life to be successful or make good money. I don't believe this at all, I think the sad reality of it all is that most people are stuck pursuing jobs they do not enjoy. A key reason for this could be because we potentially can't afford to lose the job, we fear not getting another, we are comfortable, or we're doing it for money over happiness and well-being.

At the time of writing this book, I've worked at IHOP for almost 4 years. Have there been days that were bad, stressful, and hard? Oh of course, but I overall love the job and am happy there. As you had read previously there was a time I became unhappy and was upset with Joules (my general manager) and left to go to work at another restaurant (The Nook). It took for me to leave and have time to cool off, think, and realize how much I truly loved working there.

It also taught me multiple things: being a server there, how to be patient, how to work under a stressful or chaotic situation in an efficient manner, and how to communicate with my coworkers in an effective way without degrading or talking down to them. I was able to appreciate what IHOP had brought forth to the table for me.

Once I was able to think and cool down, I was able to call Joules and elaborate on my feelings and why I was upset and left in the first place. He was able to see where I was coming from and grasp an understanding of my point of view on the situation and apologize. This helped me learn to communicate more effectively, especially with tough conversations.

November 1st, 2023

The day after Halloween I hung out with friends all day. Later that night we went to one of my favorite coffee shops (other than Starbucks) called Coffee Rush. I usually get one of their blended drinks, sugar free with almond milk, honey, and their fresh whipped cream. It is amazing. One of my friends had run to the bathroom while the rest were ordering their drinks. I was patiently waiting by the coffee station where all the straws, napkins, sugars and water were located.

As I was waiting for a guy to grab a packet of Splenda. I had this instant urge without even thinking twice and I said, "Use Stevia instead, it's better for you, less added chemicals." He looked at me and said, "Which one is Stevia?" I responded with a smile, "The green one". He set the yellow Splenda packet back down and took a Stevia packet and walked away with his coffee. I don't know why that whole interaction made me so happy. I think it made me happy because sometimes you realize you can't change the whole world, but you can change the world one person at a time, and that was a beautiful example of that.

It's the little shifts, those little 2-inch shifts, that make a difference in you and your life. Switching processed creamer for milk and honey, switching walking for an hour to jogging for 20 minutes, switching getting the venti drink at Starbucks to a grande or tall. These little shifts seem small and ineffective, but over time these little shifts in your life will all shift into a new outcome.

It's the same if you push yourself to be better every day. Instead of putting your dish in the sink and walking away, why not rinse or hand wash it so you don't leave it for the next person to do later? Or maybe when you start telling yourself you are going to do something, you actually follow through and do it? Follow through always.

These little changes and shifts in your life will become habitual and make you better and better every day. Keep your word with yourself to build that trust in yourself. Be able to trust that when you tell yourself you're going to do something tomorrow you are actually going to go ahead and do it, don't just push it again to the next day.

Most people do this, so you're not alone. Telling yourself you are going to do a task and get lazy or make an excuse to do it another time is pretty common among us all. Why not be different? If you're different you stand out, if you stand out in a positive way, you get followers, if you get followers you become a role model. Be an example, be the change, be a leader!

7

THE ROLE MODELS

There are going to be so many people who come and go out of your life. Some will leave a mark, some will leave a handprint, and others will leave you different than before you even met them. Role models don't have to be people who are well-known to the public, but they can be, such as singers, influencers, CEOs, etc. Many people say that the role-models in their lives are their parents. While others may say friends, teachers, or strangers.

Some people meet their role models, and the conversations they have with them may cause them to be inspired. Others may be inspired by their actions, and some inspired by their credentials. Everyone is different when it comes to the term "Role-Model" and to be honest, I don't think there is a specific definition. I think that role models are defined differently for everyone. A role model to me is someone who has caused a shift in my life, has caused me to view life differently, has caused me to shift to a different focus or path then I was before to better myself.

ABUNDANCE IN ABEER

I remember when I went to this family dinner. It was one of those dinners where my mom grew up with the family and they are so close to us that they become a part of my family. My mom and I had gotten there a lot earlier than everyone else, and there was Abeer with her sister. She had slowly started asking me and my mom questions about ourselves that went on for a few minutes until I asked her, "What do you do for work?" Abeer responded "I'm an emotional healer." I opened my eyes wide and gasped. I responded in curiosity "Oh my goodness, that is so cool. So, what does your job entail?"

Abeer went on about how she has sessions in her studio where people come and pay her to heal them from within. She clears out any negative energy or blockages one might have. She said she also does past life regression where she heals you from your past and even does remote healing over zoom for anyone who cannot attend her office.

I was so fascinated by everything she was sharing because I had never met anyone like her. You don't meet many people like that at all, and if you do, they do not speak as calmly about it as she does. She then started focusing more on my mom. She was asking her about her life, her job and such. My mom was going on about how I can't hear very well in my right ear and that I was born that way. Abeer started asking more about my hearing problem and if it's a certain frequency I can't hear or in general.

My mom elaborated how it's so weird because I can't hear a certain frequency completely at all, but all the other frequencies are fine. Abeer paused, looked at my mom and questioned "Nancy, what happened when you were pregnant with Jayla?"

My mom just started bursting into tears, I was so confused. I mean I had known a lot of stuff happened with my dad and her, there was a lot of emotional and physical abuse going on, but I couldn't pinpoint what Abeer meant by that, but clearly my mom did. Abeer began again as my other family members were comforting my mom. "The screaming that was going on at the time you were pregnant with Jayla was very consistent, so as she grew in your tummy, she learned to tune out that frequency of noise to cope with the trauma." This made my mom cry even harder, but it made sense and needed to be said.

It made a lot of sense. My mom went through so much with my dad and always spoke so highly of him. She told me only good things until I was about 19 or 20. Then she really sat and told me everything that went on between them in depth. It was shocking and took a lot of time for me to process because it sounded like a whole different person than what my mom had been telling me all my life about my dad. I don't know if it's a good or bad thing that I don't necessarily view him differently or love him less, but it disappoints me to a great extent.

I always had this picture in my head of him that he was perfect, funny, handsome, caring, loving, and loved by everyone around him. While he was, he also did horrible stuff to my mom as well. He was dealing with his own traumas and battles that hadn't gotten resolved as he grew up and he seemed to unleash it out onto my mom. It's hard to think about how whenever my mom and I have gone to see a psychic or go to psychic readings, they have always told my mom there's a tall man in her presence that's asking for forgiveness. They then describe to my mom how my father looked, tall and bald. My mom has always said she will never forgive him for what he did, ever. I have even sat and tried to convince her of it and she said, "He hurt me so bad, I will never forgive him, and he can pay for that wherever he is."

Aside from all of this we left the family gathering and I ended up scheduling to go see Abeer and have a session with her. It was amazing! At the end of it she had asked me if I wanted to go ahead and help her with her social media and possibly travel with her. I told her to her face I would love to, and I was interested. Then after that I never messaged her.

After many months, I sent her a message when I was traveling in Egypt asking her if she knew anything about Crypto and how I want to get into investing in stocks. It was a message I had copied and pasted to multiple people that I felt would have some sort of knowledge on the topic and would be able to help me. Abeer did not respond until a month or so later. She responded with the following text:

"Hello Jayla. Are you back yet? I just noticed your text back for July 9th> I was traveling and totally spaced out and never answered you. Sorry about that."

I was so happy to hear from Abeer considering the last time I spoke to her was almost 6 months prior. I thought she was possibly upset. I never reached out to her about working with her like I had told her. I was so excited, and I responded around the day of my arrival back home with the following text:

"Hi Abeer! How are you? I'm well. I'm currently in Egypt and will get back pretty late tonight. I would love to meet up and catch up if you're down?" She responded way faster this time around, within the hour:

"Hello gorgeous Jayla, Of course I'm down safe travels, rest and when you adjust to the time difference connect with me and we can make time to meet. Love and light your way."

Once I got back home, I reached out to meet with Abeer at a lunch spot. I updated her on my life as well as she did. She ended up asking me again about the social media topic and this time I told her yes and meant it. I elaborated to her that this is definitely something I want to do and help her with and that I have always wanted to. But at the time of her asking me I was not ready or felt like I could take on that role to my full potential or ability. Abeer was very understanding, and from then on, we started to take off.

I started by meeting up with her every Wednesday and we would talk about our future plans to have a group healing. She trusted me with passwords to her social media, she gave me a phone of hers to respond to her clients, and she just fully trusted me. It was such an amazing feeling to think she was giving me so much because she truly trusted me.

I then started to help her with her Instagram and engaged with other accounts and people similar to her, such as emotional healers and QHHT practitioners, because Abeer is a level 3 practitioner. As we started to meet up weekly, we got much closer and became friends. She even drove all the way to my Ihop work at 6 AM just to eat and see me, which was a 40 minute drive for her, and it meant so much to me.

I observed and retained so much personal information from her that I told her I knew exactly what she would like to eat for breakfast, and she replied "Oh yea? What do you think I should get then?" She shared with a shocked giggle. I stated "A quick two egg combo, with two eggs over medium, two turkey bacon, and multi grain toast with no butter. It comes with hashbrowns but knowing you, you would like the crispy potatoes better so I would suggest switching out the hashbrowns for that. Along with a side of Cholula." I started in confidence and finished off with a smile. Abeer laughed and said "You know what? That sounds perfect. I'll take that." Once her food came out she loved it, and told me how observant I am and how I have really good judgment.

When her event ended up taking place, there weren't as many people as she wanted. Abeer wanted to have about 35-40 people to attend but 20 showed up. We were actually happy about it though because there was no way she was going to be able to heal that many people in the amount of time we had booked for the space of the event. It was the perfect number of people, and she paid me like she said she would. She also said when I graduate college she wants to hire me full time, and honestly that is something I would love to do.

Abeer is very different from other people, she has been through so much in her past and so many people wronged her, but oh my gosh she is so giving. She is not in it for the money but rather to bring value to others and that is one big thing she has taught me. I want to help others and bring value to their lives like she does. She wants to help people for the better and make an impact on their lives to bring out their full potential. She is so intelligent and patient, and I admire that about her.

Abeer and I ended up becoming busy in our own personal lives and paths. I was finishing up school and she was getting back-to-back clients and bookings, I was so proud of her. Although we kind of drifted apart we still stay in touch with each other via Instagram and text and support each other. I know that we each took valuable information from each other and learned a lot from one another and I will forever be grateful for Abeer.

TONY ROBBINS

Yesterday I got off work from my 5am shift and I was wiped out. I'm usually a really go go go person. But something about yesterday had me wiped out. Instead of sitting down and scrolling through my phone at meaningless videos wasting my time I decided to watch a documentary to inform myself as I regain my energy.

As I was scrolling at documentary options, I came across this video that said "Tony Robbins: I Am Not Your Guru". My mom said, "Oh Tony Robbins!" I said, "Who's Tony Robbins?" Although the name sounded very familiar, I couldn't quite put my finger on it. Then my mom looked at me and continued "Tony Robbins is a motivational speaker he has helped many people around the world, I think you would really like that documentary." I replied "Okay yea that sounds good". I went ahead and began the documentary.

My mom popped in and out to watch it with me, but she was doing her own thing around the house. May I just say, it made me feel something inside of me I have not felt before. I felt for the people he was having one on one conversations with. The way in which he asks questions to people, makes and holds eye contact, keeps it real with them. It's so admirable. He finds a way to connect with them on a deeper level. He does not talk at surface level, he dives deep. He is someone that has inspired me. This is just the beginning of me knowing about Tony, but I strive to be like him and help others.

You can see he truly cares and cares to spread love because he says we have so much love to give. He hugs the people, he helps, and gives them a kiss on the cheek. He is full of positive radiant energy. There are not many people like him. He has found his life purpose and it's such a deep purpose that it pushes him to continue to improve, learn, and strengthen his skills every day. The key really is to find your life purpose to the core. We may have various life purposes, but finding one you enjoy and that is unique to you, and pursuing it day in and day out. That's what I want, to help others and connect with others like Tony Robbins.

MICHELLE MAY

If you haven't heard of Michelle May, she is basically a big deal. She is a past yo-yo dieter and has written a book called "Eat What You Love And Love What You Eat". Anyways I had heard about her and her book for the past few years and kept seeing her name pop up on my feed on social media, or her book ads. I follow a lot of health influencers and Michelle promotes health and wellbeing.

Anyways since I have a minor in health and nutrition, I developed a love for nutrition and enlightening others on nutrition options as well. When I was signing up for my last semester of classes I saw a class that was labeled "Mindful Eating", and I was instantly hooked. I added it to my class cart, and when I saw who the instructor was, I was beyond stunned. It was Michelle May! The book I had to rent for this mindful eating class was the book she wrote "Eat What You Love And Love What You Eat". Instead of going ahead and renting the book for the semester I saw it as a sign to go ahead and purchase it.

Once the class started one of our first assignments was an awareness journal. Michelle essentially wanted us to go ahead and document 3 days of eating in a row at least one meal per day and see if we noticed any patterns. I decided I wanted to analyze my eating patterns more in depth, so what I did was track my food for three days in a row, but I tracked every meal so I could get the best analysis of my overall eating patterns.

In essence, there were various columns and rows to fill out for each meal:

- The time of eating.
- Why am I eating?
- When am I eating?
- What am I eating?

- How do I eat?
- How much am I eating?
- Where do I invest the energy?

I thought this awareness journal was amazing. I did it for 3 days in a row and tracked every meal because I wanted an in-depth analysis. This is what I gathered and found:

1. I tend to eat more based on cravings rather than real hunger.
2. I eat smaller portions and restrict myself because of "calories" and fear of weight gain. It is good to be mindful but at the same time not because I am never satisfied or full. I restrict myself which in retaliation leads me to have more food cravings and still thinking about food.
3. I eat when I'm bored or do not have something to do to keep me busy.
4. I eat because I have a scarcity mindset, "When will I have this meal again?" "When will I be able to eat this again?" I worry I will miss the opportunity to ever have this meal again, especially if it is at an event, a friend's house, or even just a restaurant.
5. I tend to eat at a moderate pace, which is a lot better than fast, but because I worry my food will get cold or I do not have time, I tend to always feel that I'm on a time crunch. I'm still learning to be more present in the moment and focus on what is in front of me (such as my meal) instead of the thinking about the next meal, next event, or if I will have enough time to do what I need or want to do in the day, which makes me constantly anxious. I'm always thinking about something other than my food.

This awareness Journal that Michelle May created really helped me to be more mindful. Since I have done that journal, I have decided I am going to start to be more aware of my hunger/fullness cues and if it is more so to pass time, emotional comfort, or scarcity mindset.

I think something that may help me with this is always keeping a healthy snack on hand, so I don't have to worry about "scarcity" of food. It is important to figure out the root of problems, weaknesses and struggles so you're able to apply solutions to combat these problems.

In regards to my "pass time" triggers, I will be finding new ways to keep myself busy. Get up and journal, go for a walk, meditate, do some form of self-care, listen to music and dance. I love all those activities and I often try to incorporate them in my day but find that I never have enough time to complete it. Yet, I have enough time to eat when I am not hungry to "pass time" or on down time. I can use that time to do an activity I love and raise my mood. For my emotional comfort triggers, I think I'm finding better ways to cope like talking to a friend or doing an activity with loved ones.

It's hard to not think about food sometimes when you are going through a hard time and growing up it was always your way of comfort. Your mind almost naturally turns to food and wanting food because it has been embedded into your mind and body as a habit. Just like I said earlier on in the book, habits can be good and bad. While it may be hard to break a bad habit, it is possible. We tend to become comfortable with our bad habits and do them unknowingly automatically without realizing because it has become custom. The way I'm going to change this, is the moment the thought of food pops up in my head when I'm not hungry, I'm going to be aware, acknowledge the thought, and move on to an activity or a different thought.

THE ONE AND ONLY NANCY EMBABY

Nancy Embaby, where do I begin, the one and only, my mother. I know many people say that their role model may be their mother or father, but when I tell you my mom is and will continue to be my role model, she will and is my role model.

My mom raised me when she was at her lowest and highest points in life. She never wanted to let me see her weak because she wanted to show me that in life you can handle anything that comes your way. I remember growing up I used to cry a lot. She paid no mind to it. I would scream, cry or even have moments where I slammed the door. She never gave in. She did not accept that behavior in any shape or form and constantly reminded me that if I wanted to act immature, she would treat me as such.

As I grew older, I felt she was a little strict on me, although it definitely paid off. Without her, I wouldn't be anywhere close to where I am. I am her; she is me. She is the outline to my heart. She has always given me unconditional love regardless of the decisions I made. The love and protection she gave me all my life made me feel safe, secured and nurtured.

My mom is one of the strongest people I know. She has had it rough time and time again yet stands right back up to walk through whatever fire comes her way, and she does it so flawlessly and effortlessly. My mom is confident, kind, smart, caring, sympathetic, honest, blunt, a genuine leader, a mentor, and an overall an amazing human.

I am beyond blessed to have a mom like mine. She has given me tough love, always told me that there is a solution to every problem, and even helped calm me down to find a solution. She has blessed me with so much. She is my world; all I want is to give back to her HALF of what she has given me. My mom is strong, and I am strong, disciplined, focused, and driven because of her. She also supports and trusts my judgment and choices. I remember a time I was struggling really bad in school and she looked at me and said, "Jayla, you just be the best Jayla that you can be and that will ALWAYS be enough". That has stuck with me ever since, day in and day out I strive to be the best version of myself, and that's what I aspire to teach you, be the BEST you that you can be, and it will in fact ALWAYS be enough.

CHAPTER
8

THE GYM LIFE

I know exactly what you are thinking if you don't go to the gym or are new to the gym, it gives you anxiety. It's like, you want to go but you do not know where to start or your feeling judged or perhaps even unmotivated. I think that the hardest thing when it comes to the gym is where to start. So, I'm going to drop down some easy workouts that can help you get started and share workouts that helped transform my body.

When it comes to working out there are no rules. I think whatever makes you feel good and keeps you coming back to the gym is key, consistency OVER perfection. If you do intense workouts that you do not enjoy, the probability of you going back is low and it will be hard to continue keeping up and staying consistent with it. That is why oftentimes when individuals start a challenge or diet and keep going, it's because they are motivated, eager and excited for results. Yet, over time it gets tiring, and you lose that motivation to do what you set yourself up for. What do you do when the motivation dissipates what is left?

Discipline will always be the finest component to achieving anything, even over motivation. Motivation comes and goes, but discipline is something that is built and constructed into your everyday life. Discipline is something we perform even when we are unmotivated.

We do it because we said we would, we are there because we said we would be there, we arrive at 5:00PM, not at 5:40, not at 5:25, not even 5:02, because we said we would be there at 5:00.

It is about following through and training yourself and mind that you are going to get done what you said would get done because it needs to get done. Most people get motivated and excited for a new task or goal, but over time that excitement will go away or not be as strong and all you will be left with is discipline. When you are left with that discipline you know that you will still be able to finish and achieve that goal because you said you would, and you have trained your body and mind so that you do not accept anything less.

A big part of discipline is self-trust in my opinion. I think we learn to trust our word and self when we say we will do something tomorrow and know that in fact we will. A great deal of the time we often find that when we say we will do something tomorrow, we are just putting it off because we are feeling lazy or unmotivated to do it today. There is no better time to do anything than right now. Doing things today may seem like a load but it will make tomorrow easier; work hard now that way you can relax later.

A workout that helped me with my body was something I call the Cardio Quarter. What is it you may ask? Well, it's 15 minutes of 4 different cardio machines. You can start at whatever resistance level you want that you feel is best for you so it does not seem intimidating, hard, or stressful.

The whole idea is to just start somewhere at your pace and your activity level, then whenever you are ready or feel it has gotten easier, just simply increase the resistance a level up higher. There is no rule to how long you have to stay on a certain resistance level before you should move on to the next, everyone is different. I think the whole purpose is to do it because you enjoy it and it keeps you coming back to the gym and feeling good again. Consistency over perfection.

What I do at the gym is:

15 Minutes Elliptical, on Level 16.
15 Minutes Bike, on Level 13.
15 Minutes Stairmaster, on Level 7.
15 Minutes Treadmill, starting on Level 10.

When it comes to the treadmill, I have a resistance incline to start on, then every 3 minutes, I increase the incline one level higher. For example, I start the treadmill at speed 3, inclined at 10. Once it hits the 3-minute mark I go up to incline 11, then at the 6-minute mark I go up to incline 12, 9-minute mark would be incline 13, 12-minute mark would be incline 14, then you would finish that to the 15-minute mark, and you would be done with the treadmill. I have found this workout extremely effective. I have watched shows doing this workout on my phone, listened to motivational podcasts, talked to friends or family members on the phone or even jammed out to some music.

After I finish the Cardio Quarter, I pick a muscle group I would like to work on for the day. We cannot just do cardio and not do any strength training! For example, I might pick to work on Triceps. I will go to the Triceps dip machine and set it on a weight, do 5 sets. I start with say 100 lbs., it will look like this:

Set 1: 15 reps of 100.
Set 2: 12 reps of 105.
Set 3: 9 reps of 110.
Set 4: 6 reps of 120.
Set 5: 3-6 reps of 125.

If an hour of cardio a day for 4 days a week seems too much for you, I have a modified version that is just as effective. For 4 days a week I have started doing this workout method as well:

I pick 2 cardio machines and do 15 minutes of them each, then pick a muscle group to lift with for 30 minutes. In total I would be at the gym for a total of an hour a day. Here's an example of what this would look like:

Arrive to the gym at 7:02 AM:

- 15 minutes Stairmaster (Level you prefer)
- 15 minutes Treadmill (Incline you prefer, increase incline one level higher every 3 minutes)
- Post cardio I have 30 minutes to do any strength training/ weightlifting I would like
- Do a Squat rack 50 lbs. on each side, 5 sets. The next time I go to the gym and use the Squat Rack I put 55 lbs. on each side. This will help me slowly increase my weight while staying consistent and not really feeling it and will help me overall stay consistent at the gym which is what we want overall.
- The 5 sets would look like this:
    Set 1: 10 reps of 50 lbs.
    Set 2: 9 reps of 50 lbs.
    Set 3: 8 reps of 50 lbs.
    Set 4: 7 reps of 50 lbs.
    Set 5: 6 reps of 50lbs.

This will have you focusing on one weight for the day, and you will notice it feeling easier and lighter, so then the next time you arrive at the gym to do the squat rack with 55lbs. You will not struggle as much even if you are feeling unmotivated.

After doing that strength training workout you will notice that you have around 15-20 minutes left until you have to leave so pick another machine or strength training with the same set up. (5 sets of preferred starting weight throughout all reps, starting at 10 first rep going down a rep each time). Once the time hits 8:02 you can leave, do a little stretch, or stay a few more minutes if you are feeling motivated and excited to. I feel this workout template I have made myself has helped me stay not only consistent at the gym but helped me get excited to hit a new PR (Personal Record). Although it is small, it will grow into something big.

I will be able to gradually get stronger and withhold more weight for a longer time than 3 reps. I think this workout helps a lot with discipline and endurance.

Being Disciplined enough to get up and go to work out will help switch your mindset from "I have to work out" to "I get to work out" There are people all around the world who would wish to be in your shoes, have legs, have food, have a gym membership or even a car to get there. Overall, be grateful.

IT ALL STARTS NOW

I get it, starting something new or out of your routine is hard. Most of us fear change. But change is essential to growth. Change in the gym for example, even if its small changes, small changes in the weight, increasing it a little day by day, week by week, or even month by month. The smallest changes can cause the greatest effects.

Like I've said previously, there is no better time to start anything than right now. We need to get started and do the things we have been waiting and wanting to do. I do not think that waiting or making excuses for anything is beneficial to you. If you get used to making excuses now, you will forever make excuses later as well.

Make yourself accountable, be able to count on yourself, be able to trust yourself. When you tell yourself you are going to do something make sure you 110% do it. If you told yourself you are going to go to the gym tomorrow and then tomorrow rolls around and you do not do it because you are tired or decided you do not want to, then you will start to form a cycle of not being able to trust yourself when you say you are going to do something. This is important when it comes to the gym. Some days we are going to be tired, and those days are going to be hard to push, but that is when you especially need to push yourself, on the days you do not want to.

Pushing yourself when you're at your lowest, laziest, or weakest will build you up not just mentally, but physically and emotionally. You will be able to withstand more discomfort. Whether that be a change of plans, change of routine, or a hard hurdle in your life, you will start to build a keep moving forward and keep going attitude. You have to go through tough things in life to learn. You have to push yourself to grow, and you have to follow through to get to where you want to be. You do not have to be the most fit, the best looking, or have the best outfit to be a winner. You just have to be the most consistent, and that goes for everything in your life. Be consistent.

ACCEPT AND CONTINUE

When it comes to working out, you will find yourself body checking to see if all the working out is paying off. While that is all normal, make sure to be mindful of not being too hard on yourself. Some days you are going to look in the mirror and you are going to be so happy with where you are, and other days you are going to be really frustrated. Making sure that these thoughts you put into your head don't affect the rest of your day is a must. Sometimes constant body checking can result in us knit-picking things about ourselves that we do not like, or wish was different. In reality you should be doing the opposite.

Weight fluctuates, and it will forever fluctuate. There will be times when you go up a few pounds and times when you go down a few pounds, that's why it's important to stay consistent. When you look at yourself in the mirror, you may not be exactly where you want to be physically with your fitness goals. That's okay, just know staying consistent at whatever you are doing will change that. The last thing you want to do is beat yourself up about your body or have negative thoughts and stop whatever progress you were making.

In these times of insecurity when it comes to your body just remember that many factors come into play when it comes to weight such as sleep, exercise, sugary beverages, etc. In addition, sleep is such an influential factor on our health in the mainstream of things. When we lack sleep, it is what causes us to have more cravings, less energy, and not be able to concentrate.

Just know it's human to feel these negative emotions wherever you are on your health and wellness journey and you're not alone. All of the fitness guru's you follow or aspire to be on social media have days like these as well. While it may seem impossible to imagine because their disciplines and body seem unstoppable, under all that and behind a social media screen is a human who has days of insecurity just like you. Despite that, the way these fitness influencers flourish in their body and goals is they do not let these bad self-image days stop them. While it may set them back, they acknowledge, accept, and continue what they are doing. As we have spoken about before, consistency over perfection. They show up day in and day out for themselves regardless of how they are feeling because they are determined to hit their goals.

This is the mindset you should have. Know there will be setbacks. Your health and wellness journey is not just going to be smooth sailing from here and the sooner you are able to realize and understand this, the easier it will be for you to develop a strong disciplined mindset to continue on reaching those goals. When you look at yourself in the mirror and you're upset with how your body looks because of all the hard work you have put into it, do not beat yourself up, that's the worst thing you can do.

Self-talk is so powerful, so you need to make sure you speak kindly to yourself especially when you are feeling down about yourself. Simply just take a second to reevaluate, by asking these simple questions?

- Have I been sleeping 8 hours every night?
- Have I been consuming more sugary beverages than usual? Or a lot of sugary beverages?
- Have I been snacking?
- Have I been mindful when I'm eating?
- Have I been eating out a lot?
- Have I been staying active and keeping my body moving?

Once you ask yourself these questions, switch things up for the upcoming week to adjust, then at the end of that week re-evaluate yourself again.

At the end of the day, it does not matter what the number on the scale looks like as long as you're staying active, eating mostly whole foods, getting proper sleep, and limiting sugary beverages and most of all feeling good in your body.

If every time you go through one of these funks you sit here and talk down to yourself, you will eventually start to believe it. You tell yourself something enough times you will believe it. This is a main reason why people who are insecure struggle. They pick out things about themselves and talk negatively, so make sure, ESPECIALLY in times of vulnerability, you speak softly and kindly to yourself.

EAT TO LIVE, DON'T LIVE TO EAT

I remember when I gained 6 pounds for the first time in my life when I stayed the same weight all through high school. I realized I needed to make a shift because I didn't want to "let myself go". Once I did that, I used an app to start tracking calories and its true, it did more harm than good. I think the minute I started tracking my calories I realized I switched from being an intuitive eater to thinking about my next meal all the time.

Ever since then I have concluded that I do not like or agree with diets. I believe in lifestyle changes. I think that if more people were more educated on nutrition and wellbeing and were willing to listen, they would then be able to make healthier decisions for themselves.

There are so many new trends and fad diets that come out that everyone just follows the crowd to hop on and try. People are looking for instant results, which in reality is the easy way out. The best things in life are the ones we take time to achieve. The problem with society is they are constantly craving and looking for instant results. Rather than gradual, gradual results are when we learn the most as well as enjoy ourselves the most.

I think after I learned how important it is to be consistent in lifestyle choices instead of restricting and dieting. I decided to work on stopping making comments in my head about others' lifestyle choices. It's hard, it's hard to come to this conclusion on your own, but as we talked about back in chapter 2, a diet is no way to live, a lifestyle is. I never realized when I would judge others' diets and habits, however because of my personal experience I tend to reflect and look at others and I can tell who is struggling with their diets and who are not.

You only live once at the end of the day, so do, do eat, and feel how you want. Everything in moderation is key. Do not deprive yourself. Your life is supposed to be fun, beautiful, and free, so make it that way. It's never too late, as I always say the best time to start anything is right now.

When you're in a funk it may feel hard to continue sometimes, the doubts sound real doubtful, the negative self-talk sounds louder than usual, and as for your consistency, motivation and discipline you can completely throw those out the window while you're at it, they are not even there. Now when I wrote this book, I had lived a happy, safe, and freely blessed life (I still do) although I seem to be going through one of those "hard times". Let me tell you it has really put things into perspective for me.

I have always told people who have been struggling to just meditate and journal. It will help you, and if you do it consistently it will fix everything but honestly that's so far from the truth. As I've been struggling through this tough time, I have come to the realization that it's not just journaling and meditation, it's a mixture of a bunch of things:

- Mindset
- Working out/moving more
- Eat healthy
- Getting enough sleep
- Social interactive and laughing with others
- Journal and Meditating
- Lowering your screen time
- Developing a morning routine
- Being present
- Being grateful
- Practicing self-love with affirmations
- Being proactive instead of reactive

When it comes to the key to happiness, it's a choice. You choose to be grateful, you choose to be present, you choose to eat healthier, you choose to work out or take a walk, you choose to hang with friends/family more, you choose to build a morning routine, you choose to start journaling and meditation, you choose to put your phone down, and you choose to accept yourself while being proactive to achieve this change rather than reactive.

Now when I talk about being proactive and reactive to change, what do I mean? Well, when a person is reactive, they often are set off by things and play the blame game. They may say things like "This always happens to me", "I can't help it", or "I have to do it this way". Typically, people who are reactive don't take criticism very well, blame others and don't take accountability. They just wait for things to happen to them then react in a negative way over and over again.

Proactive people seek to find how to fix the issue. They may say things like "I acknowledge this way is not working so I'm going to try this way instead", "I can control my feelings", or "I will find a new way". They have a different outlook of being productive in achieving the solution/goal. Once you understand that there are things in life you can't control, you are able to let go and not let it interfere with you and your life.

BREAK-UPS ARE HARD

We often get caught up in things we can't control such as someone ghosting you. You don't know why they just stopped talking to you out of nowhere. You end up just sitting around all day anxiously waiting and hoping for a response/text as to what happened and why they went MIA. Eventually you may realize you may not ever get a response, so what's the best thing to do for you and your mental health? That is what you need to think about.

You need to always put yourself first. You can't help others if you can't help yourself. Sure, it would be nice for that closure, or getting an explanation of what happened, or what you did wrong. Or maybe so badly hope they have an amazing excuse that justifies them being away so long. However, these are just ideas that are constantly popping up in your head to try to make sense of what is going on. The need for "closure" is just an excuse.

Closure is an excuse to talk to the person again, whether it's to convince them of something, see them, hear their voice, anything. Think about it: have you ever felt better after having a "closure" talk? No not really, if anything it makes you feel worse. Typically, either way it's over so why do you care for the reasons why? Just close that door, regardless of what they did, said, told, portrayed, or whatever it seemed. You are above that and stronger than that. No one should ever make you feel unsure or anxious, if they truly cared for you. I'm not going to sit here and act like it's easy, it's not. But I'm telling you it's far easier to let go and cut those loose ends then sit here and wait for a response, or a closure talk.

Life is all about choosing your hard. If you're overweight that's hard, or if you're super fit that's hard to maintain. It's up to you in the hard you choose. Think about it, do you want to sit in a relationship that constantly has you feeling anxious, not good enough, overwhelmed, or insecure? Or would you rather leave, learn, and grow. Both are hard so choose your hard. Take these unfortunate circumstances and make yourself stronger from it. You will be able to read the signs better, you will grow, and you will move on. Most importantly, never invest your happiness in someone. A human being should never be your main source of happiness.

Happiness is found within yourself, and if you can't find that, you need to do a huge self-reflection and work on finding it within yourself. It all starts with applying self-growth steps to a better you. Sometimes you may feel hopeless, and all you want is that person, and it sucks, and it's hard, and it feels like no one understands. But they do, in their own way.

You may feel like you don't even have the strength to leave for whatever reason, because you're comfortable, you love them, you think they will change etc. but you do have the strength. You're better off on your own if someone is going to make you feel all these negative emotions. You don't deserve it, take it, leave it, and use it to make you grow. We need to go through stressful hard situations to be able to learn and grow.

Just like we put stress on our bodies at the gym so our muscles can grow, we put stress on our brains at school so we can become smarter. We go through stress in life so we can learn and grow as well. During a rough time like a break-up, it's almost essential to recognize that this is happening for you, not to you, it's all a part of your success story. It's hard to be going through a hard time in a relationship, whether you broke up, or coming close to it because you're unsure, it's all hard.

Most people tend to hide what's going on from friends and family because they don't want them to look at their significant other a certain way, if they choose to stay. Which is really sad if you think about it. If you feel that if you tell your loved ones about this awful argument or thing your significant other did and are worried about them telling you to leave, this should raise a big flag to you that they probably shouldn't be doing/ speaking to you in that way.

LONELINESS

May I first just say, it's normal to feel lonely sometimes. Some people feel lonelier than others and that's okay. I have heard so many times from people:

"It's bad if you feel lonely or sad when you're by yourself. You should be able to be happy by yourself, that's how you know if you're truly happy with yourself, when you're by yourself or not". Or I have heard "It's normal to feel lonely by yourself because humans need human interaction. That's how they feel loved, valued, and happy". Now I personally feel both statements are correct in their own ways.

Sometimes when we feel lonelier than usual, it could be a sign we are struggling internally and may be craving human interaction, laughter, and adventure more than usual. What I'm saying is I think a sign of being lonely is that you may be lacking something in your life. You may be overthinking, feeling that you have nothing to do, or just wanting to be distant from people because you're struggling in your personal life. Whatever it may be, recognize it.

I noticed when I had a time of loneliness, it was always when I was by myself. It was just me and my dog as my family was on a trip for my sister's volleyball tournament. I couldn't go because I had to work and watch the dog. Now, while I knew I could go out after work, I chose not to because I didn't want my dog to feel lonely, resulting in me feeling lonely as well. I was in this big house with my dog, no noise, no people, no nothing. You may be wondering why I hadn't invited some friends over or taken my dog out somewhere. I was actually trying to heal my voice and I was recovering from the flu. I knew if I invited friends over it would not help heal my voice and I had a lot of talking to do that weekend because I was a server.

If I were someone who had struggled with feeling lonely, or down this what I would do:

1. Go to a coffee shop, read a book there, have a coffee, do homework, smile and enjoy the noise and presence of all the people around you.
2. Go on a walk and call a friend. Just being in nature helps tremendously with any type of negative feelings and emotions. Calling a friend will make it feel like they are right there with you.
3. Go to the gym. I understand it's hard for some people to get out there and make new friends and socialize, but going to the gym is a great way to relieve any negative emotions and feelings as well.
4. Find a new hobby. As silly and cliché as this may sound, it's true. Find something that you have always wanted to do that you have been putting off, and just DO IT! There is no more explanation or elaboration to it, just do it.

Again, remember it's completely normal to feel lonely sometimes. You're a human and we have all felt lonely before. Although being aware that it's not constant again and again is crucial, this could be a sign you're feeling something more internally and your body is trying to signal to you to change it.

BE READY FOR THE WORST

Oftentimes we sit here and hold ourselves back because of the "What If" statements we devise in our head. We stress, we over think and over analyze the worst possible scenarios. I would say that does not benefit you, but it does. Overthinking does not benefit you, but analyzing the worst possible outcomes in depth does. You see, if you take any scenario that you are stressed or fearing about, for example maybe being in a relationship, and worrying they will break up with you, then you will never be able to enjoy any events life has to offer and enjoy that relationship while you can. So next time you have a negative thought and can't stop thinking about it, let your mind think about it. But this time, truly think of the worst thing that could happen in that scenario to its depths and let it play out. Once you are able to do this you will realize the "worst" scenario you were thinking of was not that bad.

Let's refer back to our breakup example. The worst scenario for you would be your partner breaking up with you. Okay so now they broke up with you and you thought your world would end and everything would fall apart, and you would never be with someone ever again. Despite that, you see how when you break up, yes you would be sad, but you would eventually move on, you would continue to eat, drink, workout, hang out with friends, work, do the things you love and enjoy. Over time you would realize that you would be able to live without them and life would go on even if you were sad. The reason it's best to play out the worst circumstances is not only so we are ready for them, but we see they are not as bad as we imagined. If we do that, we can mentally prepare for any circumstance without living in a state of anxiety inducing "what-ifs".

YOU BETTER BELIEVE IT

People are disappointing.

As simple as that statement is, it speaks volumes. I had just learned this a few months ago and it hit me deep to my core. It truly does not matter how long you have known a person, how much they love you, and whatever you guys have been through. There is always a possibility they can stab you in the back. I don't say this for you to worry but to just have awareness. People are disappointing, you never want to rely on anyone for anything that is truly important to you, rely on yourself. You want it done on time, do it yourself, you want it done exactly, do it yourself, you want it done right do it yourself.

With all that being said, what if someone you love stabs you in the back then what? Well let me tell you, it will be shocking, it will feel shocking. You will almost want to talk to them, ask them why they did what they did, why did they lie? Why didn't they tell you the truth, and quite honestly that person may not even want to talk to you because they know they are in the wrong and do not know what to say. Another word for it is "speechless' '. You will in return sit in your head when you're hurting and overthink all these thoughts such as:

- "Why would they do this to me?"
- "I just don't understand."
- "I thought they loved me."
- "We have been through so much, and they did this."
- "They told me they would never do this".

I know it hurts, but then you are going to try to convince yourself you need a closed conversation. You don't. Let it go. As we talked about earlier, closure is an excuse to talk to them more, their actions were all the closure you needed, the words mean nothing. Look how far listening to their words got you thus far. Time to release, move on, build, and grow. Use this pain and hurt to know BETTER, be BETTER, and do BETTER. You can, you will, and you are.

It's hard to believe, but time really does heal. Make sure to feel out your feelings as well. Get a journal and let your mind overthink as much as it would like during a hard time. Releasing all your emotions out on a piece of paper helps tremendously, and going back to read it the next day to re-analyze your emotions helps too. You can see why you are thinking a certain way and come to your own conclusions.

Actions speak louder than words. Analyzing what you wrote down will help you internalize what truly happened and give you the closure you need without having to speak to that person again. You are stronger than you know, the first step is believing it. Believe you are strong, being strong in a mindset is a way of acting or portraying. You can be whatever thoughts you embody of yourself, so why wouldn't you make your thoughts of yourself the most top tier thoughts imaginable.

IN CONTROL VS. OUT OF CONTROL

It's important to realize there are things we simply just have no control of in our lives. Oftentimes people think they have control over certain things or situations, and it ends up making them go mad. Once we are able to differentiate what we have control over and what we do not, we are able to live a more peaceful life.

Let's talk about things we do not have control over first: Other people, others actions, reactions, thoughts, and opinions. Government rules/ decisions, the past or the future. Now let's list what we DO have control over: Our actions, reactions, thoughts, and opinions. When you read over the two different lists for some of you it sparked some sort of light bulb moment. Although for others of you, you may feel it's "debatable".

Many people may feel that when government decisions are made, that's unfair because we do have voting or this and that and the other. Still, I put it on that list because even though we can vote and can have a say at the end of the day, the final decisions for change and guidelines are not ours. I have seen way too many people get in their head about government issues and stress themselves out, or make themselves mad and it becomes all they talk about. How is that healthy for you as an individual? It's out of your control, and you need to release it and keep telling yourself it's out of your control.

As for other people's thoughts and opinions of us, we often worry about what other people may be thinking or saying about us. We may be finding that we act a certain way around these people to be more liked and accepted. However, why would you want to do that? At the end of the day no matter how you act, or what you say or do, this person will still have an opinion about you that you cannot control. Acting in a certain way to be liked is portraying a different type of persona then who you truly are to get that validation from others. As a result of this, we see that they may end up liking us more or less but liking us more or less as a person we portray ourselves to be, that's not even truly us. We just wanted to be liked and loved and not judged in a bad way.

In view of this, we see that if we are going to be judged either way, and it's out of our control, then why wouldn't we just be our true selves. Whoever likes you stays around, and whoever does not will leave. There are people in your life that just love everything about you and all of you, while there will be others who just don't and that's fine. You will never be liked by everybody and on the other side of it, you will never be disliked by everybody either.

If we tie this into others reactions/actions a lot of the time, we could end up obsessing over it, especially if you just got out of a breakup. Many times, we are so used to being in a relationship with this person and checking in with each other to see how the other person feels about going to a certain event or hanging with certain people, that when we break up, all those boundaries are dropped. Once they are dropped you may start to hear things like your ex-boyfriend Danny may be out hanging with a girl he told you not to worry about Vanessa. While it is heartbreaking that Danny told you not to worry about Vanessa throughout the whole relationship and now, they are going on dates and hanging out as soon as you guys break up. Yet, it's out of your control.

Sometimes things that are out of our control are hard to accept, but you need to let it go. The quicker you can realize it's out of your control and accept it for what it is, the quicker you are able to live more at peace with yourself.

CHAPTER
10

IT'S YOU

Overall, you are in control. You are in control of everything that involves you in your life. If you want something bad enough you ultimately will and can achieve it. You need to want it so bad, that you will be unstoppable of any roadblock, comment, or negativity that comes your way, because it will.

Success in anything is not a straight clear desert road, it more so is like a rollercoaster that goes through a raining forest that keeps breaking down and animals, bugs, and water keep getting in front of your track. What would we do in that scenario if it was real? Well, I will tell you right now you would not just sit there in the pouring rain with a big bear in front of you saying, "Well I guess I was not meant to finish this ride". Nope you would get the heck out of that roller coaster, run away and hide until the bear leaves and the storm calms down, and find a way to distract the bear and hop back on the rollercoaster in the pouring rain and continue the ride, or fight the bear.

That is how life is, there are going to be so many obstacles that we are unable to even predict. Although, just like there are going to be so many obstacles in your life there are going to be various solutions to choose from. You just have to pick one and execute it. If the solution does not work you pick another one, until it works.

Back to the forest example, if your rollercoaster gets stopped in the rain because of the bear and you decide to go hide and wait for the rain to stop and the bear to leave and you realize the bear is not leaving and the rain is not stopping you are going to continue to just keep hiding in the woods. You are going to find a different solution because just as Albert Einstein said:

> *"The definition of insanity is doing the same thing*
> *over and over and expecting different results"*
> *—Albert Einstein.*

If you tried that solution and it did not work you may try distracting the bear, feeding the bear, or even talking to the bear. You keep trying until you can hop back on that rollercoaster and finish the ride, because you were meant to. It's the same thing when it comes to life and success. You are on this planet for a reason, and everyone has a purpose. Find your passion, learn on it, work at it, and do not stop, never stop. No matter what they say, no matter what they think, and no matter what they do. Do not listen to others advice or opinions unless they are where or who you want to be. Another good way of looking at it is if you wouldn't want to switch lives with that person and be in the position they are in then definitely don't listen to them. Humans are full of judgment, expectations and comments. Learn to not take everything to heart and have a filter on it. Grow YOURSELF and everything around you will grow, be different. The most successful and famous people grew to be amazing and make change in this world by being different. Just like Rob Dial said:

> *"Most people live mediocre lives so why would*
> *you want to be like most people?"*
> *—Rob Dial*

Furthermore, that's all everyone else does, follow the latest trends, slangs and styles. People fear standing out, they don't want eyes on them, they are stressed for judgment, but that's how you get stronger, get uncomfortable, get rejected, and put yourself in the toughest scenarios so you can grow.

Uncomfortable = Growth
Rejection = Tough skin

Grow yourself and teach yourself to not care what others are saying around you and do it regardless of their thoughts.

THE PEOPLE AROUND YOU

The top five people you surround yourself with reflects who you are. Go ahead and count the top five people you spend most of your time with, if you're not happy about it, then find some new friends or spend less time with them. You want to invest your time and energy in people who have high goals and are better than you at a certain skill you want to achieve. This will motivate you to be and get better at it.

Grow yourself, choose who you spend your time with wisely. It is so important because you have one life to live. Please do not spend it on instant satisfaction. Work hard to get to where you want to be so you can live how you want to live. I'm not saying cut all your friends off who have no goals or hold you back. I'm saying don't invest all your time in them. If you hang around friends who say they are going to do something and then don't follow through, you will end up doing the same thing. You will pick up the language, slang, mannerisms, and habits of people you spend most of your time with.

There really is no "expert" at anything. People who are "experts" just continue to grow and learn more than the average person. As long as you know at least 2% more than the people around you, you are looked at as a hard worker with much determination and knowledge. For example, if you work at a restaurant, and every time you get a big party, instead of complaining like the other servers be happy to take it. People will look up to you because you're 2% more mature than the people around you. Or if you are always going the extra mile when it comes to sweeping your section and you always sweep the coworkers section next to you, then you will be looked at as an overachiever which will inspire others to work as hard as you.

Doing little things that show personal growth, discipline, and dedication are very important. The more you show others how you put your best foot forward day in and day out, the more they will be inspired to do so as well. It will trigger the "If she/he can, I can too" effect. That being said, it's important to surround yourself with overachievers, because it pushes you harder and further than before. It is also important to notice if your friends, family members, coworkers, or anyone you see in your life are okay.

Here are top 3 tips to look out for:

Notice:

1. Tone of Voice
2. When they become quieter than usual.
3. Responding "I'm alright" or "I'm here".

1. Tone of Voice

The reason you should notice a loved one's tone of voice is because you can tell a lot just by how optimistic or aggressive their tone of voice is to you. If we reflect on a time, we were really happy we were never talking slow or sluggish. Even if we were tired from the night before and had 4 hours of sleep, and you are happy within yourself and your life you don't speak in a sluggish stand-offish manner. You will still be upbeat and happy, maybe not the minute you wake up, but a few hours into the day that tired feeling wears off. If you truly are happy and content in your life it will affect your tone of voice a great deal.

It's especially important to recognize when people seem more stand-offish, irritated or annoyed. Know that it's probably not you, they are probably dealing with their own life or self-battles in their head that in retaliation results in them taking it out on you. So be patient when you encounter those scenarios. Think about it from their perspective, if you were having a rough day the last thing you would want is someone making a comment about your attitude or starting an argument with you. You would want support and patience, so give that back to others as well.

2. When They Become Quieter Than Usual

I'm a firm believer that "I'm just tired" is simply an excuse. Not an excuse stating you aren't tired, I do believe people get tired, but it does not cause them to be in a slump all day, not laugh, or smile, or have conversation. Typically, when people are tired, they may just seem a little out of it, loopy, or even clumsy. When you notice that a loved one is quiet, try to subtly bring it up to them. If they seem annoyed by the questions just you showing you care and that you're there means the world to them, even if they show it or not. Stating things like "Just know I'm here for you whenever", and "You let me know if you need anything at all". I believe silence from the mouth is like sirens in the head. Meaning the less they speak, the more they speak internally in their heads. As we know, being alone with your thoughts never ends well. It causes overthinking and spiraling into holes, feelings, and places we do not want to be.

3. Responding "I'm alright" or "I'm here"

I think one of the biggest indicators someone is going through a rough time is when you ask them how they are doing or feeling and they respond with "I'm alright", or "I'm here". It's a steer away from the direct question and they may even try to play it off as a joke. Just be aware of those patterns, if you end up asking them again how they are doing and they state a mediocre response yet again, ask more questions.

Do NOT just carry on the conversation or whatever you were planning on asking them. Ask them "Why alright? Are you okay?" Some people may share and others may not, but either way just showing you care and that you are an ear to them if they ever need is important.

One thing to keep in mind is if they share something personal with you, do not say things like "I get it" or "I know what you mean" or flip the story onto or about you. Reason being, you don't understand. I'm sorry but you don't. You may have gone through a similar experience, and you could stay that briefly such as "I've been through a similar situation and it was tough, I'm sorry to hear that you're going through that." You do not understand what they are feeling, going though or even the details and depths of it all.

Seeing that, we never want to flip the situation onto us. So, prevent yourself from trying to tell a personal story about yourself. Often when you're going through a hard time a response such as "I'm so sorry you're going through that, I'm here for you if you need, and thank you so much for feeling comfortable enough to share that with me" is way better than 'I get it" or "I know it sucks". Be aware of that, a listening ear, a hug, or a shoulder to turn to or cry on means a great deal.

LISTEN, LEARN, AND APPLY

I believe we learn the most when we talk to the people around us. I think face to face interaction is so crucial. When we get away from surface level conversations or scripted conversations such as "How are you?" "Good, the weather today is really nice huh?" "Yea it is. The forecast said it should stay sunny and cool like this the rest of the week!" Like no, boring, and honestly we both know I don't care, you don't care, and we don't care about this conversation that much. We are just trying to pass time, get through the conversation and move on with our day.

That's why I've love being a server. I think it has really helped me to adapt social skills in a way I wouldn't have been able to without the experience I have now. The beautiful thing about it is, I have made friends working here, others would say "regulars" - customers who come in regularly and ask for you to serve them. I have had in-depth conversations with these friends and got to know and understand more about who they are as a person, what they have gone through, how they have overcome it, and how it shaped them into the person they are today.

When we reflect on previous conversations, especially ones that are with strangers, we tend to constantly think about what we are going to say next. We have a fear that it may get awkward, or silent so we are constantly thinking about what to say next, not because we are being rude and not wanting to listen, but because we are trying to prevent this moment of silence that we may face if we don't have something prepared to say on standby.

That's understandable, but when you learn to release that fear of silence, and drop your thoughts, and just focus on the present moment and the words that are coming out of the mouth of the person in front of you, and comprehend it, you will feel a lot more at peace. Why is that? If we teach our brains to stop constantly thinking about what to say next when others are talking and just truly give the person in front of us our undivided attention, we will feel more connected to the person we are speaking to. If we take in what the other person is saying and not thinking about what to say until they are finished, we are teaching our brains to focus on one thing at a time. We are focusing on the words of the person we are talking to and absorbing it.

When we listen to people's stories or what they have been through, that is when we learn the most. Think about it, all the most important discoveries of life have been made by people who had gone through something to find it. The things we learn in school about history and wars, people went through that. Stories have been passed down, books written, documentations made to prevent the same chaotic scenarios from happening. We are all human, and to help people or make a change you don't need to know everything, and you never will know everything. You can always continue to learn and grow as you help and inspire others.

When it comes to speaking with new people, try a new approach from now on, or at least give it a try. When they speak just listen and take in what they are saying. If a thought floats in your mind such as a question, ask it! And ask it unapologetically, your mind and body are signally to you they want clarification or to learn more, so acknowledge that and take it in. Our minds love to learn, we learn every day, it's healthy not just for the mind but for your wellbeing, the more you know the more you can help others the more you help others the more you help yourself.

Giving to people is the biggest reward, you get the best feeling from just knowing you helped someone out. Although, you should never do it for publicity, reputation or to look good in front of somebody. You should do it because you truly care for and want to help that person because you have the knowledge to. Listening when people are talking helps us to grasp an understanding/ perspective on things we have never felt or possibly gone through before. When we take the time to hear people out and what's happened in their life, we get a better outlook on how it changed them into the person they are today. When we listen to people's stories, we can learn how they coped or handled it in the past. We learn more for when we hear someone we have known has gone through the same scenario. We can help walk others through their feelings and thought process based on what we have learned from someone who has went through a similar issue and got passed it.

OLD RELATIONSHIPS AREN'T THE WORST

Why is it that we always try avoiding contact with people in public places? Or even when we see people we knew years back or went to school with? Why is it that we have normalized avoiding or ignoring seeing these people in public? I think many people feel it could be uncomfortable or awkward. But it's important to understand that you were meant to see that person in public, for whatever the reason be, go up and say hi. I know it can be anxiety inducing, but just taking that first step to go up and say hi to someone could turn their lousy day to a sensational one. If this sounds scary to you, that should be of all the reasons you especially should practice doing this the most.

I have a simple mindset format you can abide by when encountering these scenarios that will surely help you. We know most of what we do in a day is determined by our thought process and feelings to a certain scenario or event. So, when we go ahead and just have the "DO IT" mindset instead of thinking deeper into it, we get a lot more done.

Steps for Engaging in These "Uncomfortable" Conversations:

1. Just walk up and say "Hey!"
2. The conversation won't be long, and if it is, WHO CARES
3. Nothing will go wrong
4. Do it for THEM

1. Just Walk up and say Hey!
   - When you see a person you feel compelled to talk to, it's a sign you should. Don't think much of it, just walk up and say hi. It starts with your body, when you see them just start getting your body in the motion of walking up to start that conversation and your mind will follow.

   - Instead of giving your brain time to think if you should do it or not, the minute you start walking over there or motioning physically to do this, your mind will filter from "I don't know if I should say hi" to "Okay we are going to say hi".

   - Our brains are simply just a tool, use it as one. Your brain will follow what you tell it to do, you are in control.

2. The conversation won't be long, and if it is, WHO CARES

   - Many individuals don't want to go up and engage in conversation because of the fear of not being able to get out of it. While that is understandable, that is not a beneficial mindset to have at all.

   - Stop focusing on being so consumed on time, focus on the now and the present. Worrying about if they are going to think you're awkward or overthinking that the conversation will be awkward is not doing you any good at all.

- Go into the conversation thinking about how you want to learn more, what you can learn. Each person on this earth brings value, and has been through experiences that you haven't, so when you talk to new people you are opening a door to new knowledge, so take it in.

3. Nothing will go wrong

- Think, what is the worst that will happen if you go up and say hi? Nothing. The conversation may end quicker than you originally thought, but it won't ruin anything.

- New situations can be anxiety inducing, as well as new conversations, but we grow in uncomfortableness and new situations and scenarios.

4. Do it for THEM

- Sometimes just going up to someone saying "Hey! How you been?" can make their day.

- Some people may be going through a lot more than you know. Just acknowledging them may shed light on a dark day. So spread that love and just show you cared enough to say "hi" and are happy to see them.

CHOOSE LOVE OVER HATE

Here's the thing: we sit here and hold grudges over people who hurt us. We sit here and resent the people who betrayed us or did not support us or just left us heartbroken. The reality of it all is that it is a choice. It is a choice to choose to have love/hate for somebody.

If you are getting out of a relationship with someone and it's because you have "stopped loving them" then that is a choice. You're CHOOSING to not have love for them, you're CHOOSING to not love them. The thing is love is an unconditional term, like how a mom loves her child. She chooses to love her child no matter the choices they make in life, no matter what they do, say, the mother chooses to always love her child.

When we choose to have love for people instead of hating, it's a release in our minds. We often think if we go around hating somebody or say we hate somebody, it will just upset the person we are hating and hurt them more in return. But in reality, it's just hurting you the most. If we choose to have love for all the people around us, acknowledging the past, acknowledging the wrong doings, then we are choosing peace. We are choosing peace not only for ourselves, but for the people around us, the environment, our minds, all of it.

How good would it feel to walk into a room and say, "I love everyone here". It would feel amazing. Now you don't have to tell the person you currently hate that you are now choosing to love them, you can just internalize it, and have that love for them. We are always told to have self-love, and be accepting of ourselves, but there are some people who have done really horrific things in their lifetime, should they choose to hate themselves? No, love should be unconditional, and a choice, we can acknowledge the wrong doings, but still love deeply. We are humans and we are meant to love, so choose to love because it's a beautiful thing.

CONCLUSION

With that being said...

Wherever you live, however old you are, you were meant to receive this book. You were meant to see this book, hear about this book and overall read it. Take everything you learned in this book and incorporate it into your overall life.

There is always room for self-growth, you can never know enough information about the world and yourself. The more you know the better.

I would say what defines anyone is their actions and attitudes towards not just others but within themself. We know who we truly are under pressure and stressful situations.

I would say my goals and my mindset is what has made me the person I am. I am very driven and disciplined and when I want something I go get it regardless of what others have to say about it, this should be you too.

My purpose in life I believe is to help others to succeed within themselves and reach their goals and dreams while being the best version of their authentic self. I do so on social media through Tik Tok, Instagram, and my podcast on Spotify. I post my authentic self in hopes to inspire others to embrace all of themselves as well.

I also believe we all have a gift, a gift that is unique and unlike anyone else. We are all meant to share, teach and inspire others. You are greater, stronger and more powerful than you know. Know that whatever passions and dreams you have are truly possible. Do not let anyone tell you otherwise. People will always hate you regardless of who you are and how you act, so you may as well act as your most authentic self.

Here are some life mottos I stand by in summary to help you:

"The First Step is Being Aware" - Jayla Embaby

"It's Okay to Make Mistakes as Long as You Learn from them" – Anonymous

"Everything Happens for a Reason" – Aristotle

"Everything Happens for you, Not to you" - Byron Katie

Success is 99% failure and 1% success. You must learn about all the possible ways something can't or won't work before you figure out what does. That may look like crashing your car, losing a loved one, going bankrupt.

The most traumatic experiences in our lives are the worst yet the best thing to happen to us at the same time. They often spark change and grow, and shift us to a new outlook on life and overall, a new direction.

As far as the "No-Fluff" part of this book, if you haven't discovered what it means yet, it means "no-nonsense" or messing around.

There is a standard line that is set between us and everyone else, the bare minimum line if you will. Once you stop the nonsense and the messing around and choose to work 2% better than the people around you, you will get far in this world.

As my friend Bob taught me that I mentioned earlier on in this book, many people think you must be double better than the people around you to be noticed or successful, but that's highly impossible and highly untrue. You just have to be 2% better than people around you and do it consistently.

You are amazing, you are strong, you are unstoppable. Do not let anyone get in the way of your success. You only live once, enjoy it.

Understand that if you keep going at something consistently no matter what you will get there. I'm so happy you took the time to read this book, and I can't wait for you to take the better you off into the world.

And as my mom said,
"Be the BEST you that you can be, and that will ALWAYS be enough."

Finish dates
July 29th, 2024.

AFFIRMATIONS

Here are some affirmations I have created for you for whatever you may be struggling with that day. I repeat the list of the section you are struggling with 3 times aloud or as many times as you want, read it slowly and confidently.

ACCEPTANCE
I am accepting myself as I am right now.
I am happy with where I'm at right now.
I am feeling good about myself.
I love myself as I am.
I feel proud for how far I have come.
I am proud of myself.

SELF-CONFIDENCE
I am amazing.
I am kind.
I am smart.
I am worthy.
I am great.
I am strong.
I am confident.
I am unstoppable.
I am courageous.
I can achieve anything and everything I want.
I am capable of anything I put my mind to.
I am stronger than I know.

I can, I will, and I am.

BODY
I have a body.
I have a strong body.
I have a beautiful body.
I love my body.
I love my mind.
I love my body as it is today.
I love my body as it is.
I feel great in my body.
My body's a blessing.
I take care of my body.
I have a beautiful body.
I enjoy working out to keep my body fit.
I won't let my mind bully my body.
It's not about changing my body; it's about becoming the best person I can be.

ACHIEVING SUCCESS
I am attracting the perfect career.
I am living with abundance.
I am making a difference in this world.
I am deeply motivated to work towards my goals.
I am achieving more and more success.
I am a go-getter.
I am worthy enough to follow my dreams and manifest my desires.
I am a strong individual who attracts success and happiness.
I am worthy of my dream job and am creating the career of my dreams.

DOING YOUR BEST

I am doing my best.

I am actively pushing myself to be better every day.

I am getting better every day.

I am willing.

I am dedicated.

I am driven.

I am doing my best and that will always be enough.

I always get through any and all obstacles life throws my way.

www.ingramcontent.com/pod-product-compliance
Lightning Source LLC
Chambersburg PA
CBHW051832040426

42447CB00006B/485